Anchors in Floating Lives

Interventions with Young People Sexually Abused through Prostitution

Edited by
Margaret Melrose
with
David Barrett

Russell House Publishing

First published in 2004 by:
Russell House Publishing Ltd.
4 St George's House
Uplyme Road
Lyme Regis
Dorset DT7 3LS

Tel: 01297-443948
Fax: 01297-442722
e-mail: help@russellhouse.co.uk
www.russellhouse.co.uk

British Library Cataloguing-in-publication Data:
A catalogue record for this book is available from the British Library.

ISBN: 1-903855-21-7

Typeset by TW Typesetting, Plymouth, Devon.

Printed by Antony Rowe, Chippenham

About Russell House Publishing

RHP is a group of social work, probation, education
and youth and community work practitioners and
academics working in collaboration with a professional
publishing team.
Our aim is to work closely with the field to produce
innovative and valuable materials to help managers,
trainers, practitioners and students.
We are keen to receive feedback on publications and
new ideas for future projects.

Contents

Acknowledgements

Our most grateful thanks go to the contributors, who have been willing to share their experiences, and to their senior managers for allowing them to do so. In this respect, we are most grateful to the Home Office for encouraging positive interventions and allowing projects that they have funded to draw on the work they have done to inform best practice for others grappling with these difficult issues. Thank you.

We would like to thank Geoffrey Mann at Russell House Publishing for suggesting that we edit this book and for facilitating its production. Thank you for the opportunity. We also wish to express our appreciation to Professor John Pitts in his role as commissioning editor. His counsel, support and kindness have been both abundant and invaluable. Thank you for your support.

We would also like to thank the University of Luton for supporting us in this endeavour.

Margaret would like to convey her sincerest thanks to all her family and friends for being patient with her when she has been impatient to work on this book. Especially, thanks to Earl for putting up with the night shifts without complaint.

David wishes to acknowledge that the publication of this book is due, in no small part, to Margaret's drive, intellectual dexterity and remarkable scholarly commitment to the exploited and oppressed.

The authors of Chapter 5 wish to acknowledge the contribution of project support staff.

For Leah with love

About the Contributors

The Editors

Margaret Melrose is a Senior Research Fellow in the Department of Applied Social Studies at the University of Luton. She has researched extensively around issues of young people who are involved in prostitution and young people who are involved in drug use. She has published widely around these issues and has spoken at national and international conferences on these topics. As well as journal articles and chapters, Margaret has published *One Way Street: Retrospectives on Childhood Prostitution* (1999) (with D. Barrett and I. Brodie) The Children's Society, and *Fixing It? Young People, Drugs and Disadvantage* (2000) Russell House Publishing. She is currently managing an evaluation of projects developed to support young people involved in prostitution and funded by the Home Office. She has collaborated with David Barrett on numerous projects around the topic of young people involved in commercial sexual exploitation.

David Barrett is Professor of Applied Social Studies and Dean of the Faculty of Health Care and Social Science at the University of Luton. He has researched and published around children abused through prostitution for a number of years and edited *Child Prostitution in Britain: Dilemmas and Practical Responses* (1997) The Children's Society, and *Youth Prostitution in the New Europe* (2000) Russell House Publishing. His most recent publication, with Alyson Brown, is *Knowledge of Evil: Child Prostitution and Child Sexual Abuse in Twentieth Century England*, Willan Publishing. In addition to these books, David has published numerous journal articles on this topic. David has also acted as consultant to voluntary and statutory sector agencies as well as numerous research projects and has spoken at many national and international conferences around this issue.

The Contributors

Alyson Brown was formerly a lecturer in Criminology at the University of Luton. She is currently a lecturer at Edgehill Higher Education College and works on the history of crime and punishment. Her main areas of interest and publication are penal history and the history of child prostitution. Her co-authored book (with David Barrett) *Knowledge of Evil: Child Prostitution and Child Sexual Abuse in Twentieth Century England* was published in 2002.

Anne Byerley has experience of working in the fields of homelessness, criminal justice and mental health and is a qualified probation officer. Anne worked for South Yorkshire Probation Service for ten years and was formerly employed by Turning Point at SHED, the under 19s drug and alcohol service in Sheffield. Anne is now a drug treatment worker with North Derbyshire Community Drug Team within the NHS.

Tim Darch has been involved with gay men's health and social well being since 1994. He became aware of issues surrounding young men involved in prostitution in 1996 when he assisted a young man to exit. Since then, he has worked with vulnerable young men enabling them to gain the help they need when they need it most. He is currently Street Team Co-ordinator for Terrence Higgins Trust West.

Nicola Didlock has worked for young people's drug services for six years. She is currently employed by Turning Point as a service manager for SHED, a young person's drug and alcohol project in Sheffield. Nicola has also worked with young people in residential care and with offenders in local communities.

Susan Drinkwater is the academic lead on the 'Widening the Net' project at the University of Luton. She previously worked in practice with adolescents living in local authority residential care. Susan has extensive research experience having worked on a number of projects including services for families, support for families with adolescents and school and youth inclusion initiatives. Susan has recently worked as a researcher for a Home Office funded evaluation of initiatives dealing with sexual exploitation of young people.

Tom Duffin is a police officer with the West Midlands police. He was responsible for managing one of the two national pilots to work differently with children abused through prostitution. Tom has contributed to developing national guidance on the topic and has spoken at regional, national and international conferences on this subject. Tom has travelled to Colombia on two occasions to support new ways of partnership working with street children involved in prostitution. He has an MSc in Public Sector Management.

Di Foley is project leader at Bristol BASE. She started working for Barnardo's in 1995 as a sexual health worker. The work of the sexual health team led to the formation of BASE (Barnardo's Against Sexual Exploitation). Di is a Senior Social Work Practitioner who has worked with young people for the past 20 years. She has fostered difficult to place young people as well as working in residential homes and as a community support worker.

Helen Greenwood is the Exams Offficer for the University of Luton and is studying part-time for a Masters by research in the area of child exploitation.

Sue Gregory has worked in social services since 1981. She is currently Service Manager for Safeguarding and Quality in Nottingham City Social Services Department. Since 1997, Sue has taken a lead role in developing strategies for identifying, and intervening with, children who are sexually exploited.

Ann Lucas has worked as a social worker since 1977. In 1996, she was appointed Child Protection Co-ordinator for Sheffield City Council Social Services Department. Ann has been working with young people at risk or involved in sexual exploitation since that time.

Fiona Lothian is a qualified drama teacher and has spent the past 18 years using drama to explore various issues with young people. Fiona has worked as a youth worker for the young women's unit in Sheffield for nine years. Since February 2001, she has been involved in a project developing one-to-one support for young women at risk or involved in commercial sexual exploitation.

Nasima Patel qualified as a social worker in 1991 and worked for Bradford Social Services until 1994 when she moved to London to work for Hackney Social Services. She joined the NSPCC in 1999 to develop a service for young women at risk of, or involved in, commercial sexual exploitation. She is currently Service Manager with the NSPCC and manages the Street Matters project in London.

Jenny J. Pearce has worked as a teacher and youth worker in youth justice. Working for the School of Health and Social Science at Middlesex University, her research and publications have focused on young women, street cultures and sexual exploitation. Jenny has recently completed a two-year research project into young women and sexual exploitation, developed in partnership with the NSPCC and funded by the Joseph Rowntree Foundation.

Joanna Scammel is a part-time Senior Practitioner at Bristol BASE. She has experience of working with young people around mental health issues. Joanna has also worked in residential social work and has experience of training other social work practitioners.

Marilyn Victor-Jefferson has been working as a qualified youth and community worker for 17 years. She is currently employed by Sheffield Futures young women's unit. Marilyn has been involved in a project developing one-to-one support for young women at risk or involved in commercial sexual exploitation for two years.

Lisa Wilkinson-Shaw has worked with young people in various settings for 16 years and has extensive experience of residential work, youth justice and young people involved in prostitution. Lisa currently works for the Genesis project, Leeds where she supports and advocates on behalf of young women and girls who are sexually exploited. Lisa also works as a freelance trainer specialising in leaving care legislation, challenging behaviour and working with young people who are socially excluded.

Ian Winton has served in Nottinghamshire Police for 20 years during which time he has undertaken various duties including work in the drug squad. He is currently an Inspector in Nottinghamshire Police Anti-Vice Team.

Rowena Wood is a newly qualified social worker who worked for Bristol BASE. Jointly with a drugs worker, she undertook outreach work for the Pandora project in Bristol. Rowena has experience of working with drugs and young people and is now continuing that work in a neighbouring local authority.

Preface

For those people working with, or concerned about, the welfare of young people involved in commercial sexual exploitation, whose practices and experiences are described in this book, the Sexual Offences Act 1957 posed enormous problems because of its failure to distinguish between the children being exploited and the adults exploiting them. Moreover, the Street Offences Act 1959 failed to distinguish between children and adults engaged in prostitution. Until the introduction of government guidelines in 2000, young people could be cautioned and convicted for prostitution-related offences from the age of ten (Aitchison and O'Brien, 1997).

Even after the introduction of these guidelines, young people could still be processed through the criminal justice system if they were deemed, by those concerned with their care, to be 'persistently and voluntarily returning to prostitution' (DoH/HO/DfEE, 2000). As we have argued elsewhere, while it is true that it is the most damaged and needy young people who will be most difficult to protect, support and enable to leave prostitution, a punitive response will be even less effective (Melrose and Ayre, 2000; Barrett and Melrose, 2003). This point is reinforced in the chapter by Patel and Pearce whose case material demonstrates that it is those who are most marginalised and alienated from welfare support who are most likely to 'persist' in prostitution.

The Sexual Offences Act 2003, which received Royal Assent and became operational in May 2004, promises, in theory at least, to change all. The Act signals the government's intention to 'take effective action' against perpetrators involved in crimes of commercial sexual exploitation (Home Office, 2002: 30). It contains a new offence of 'Commercial sexual exploitation of a child' which protects children up to the age of 18 and covers the activity of 'buying the sexual services of a child'. The maximum penalties for this offence will be life imprisonment if the child is under 13, 14 years imprisonment where the child is 13–15 and seven years imprisonment when the child is 16–17 (Home Office, 2002: 30). Our expectation is that as a result of this new legislation, whether young girls are involved in selling or 'swapping' sex for drugs or other 'favours', it will be much easier to prosecute the men involved in buying their 'services'. This should apply whether young men and women are soliciting on the street – as described in the contributions from Sheffield, Leeds and Bristol – or from behind closed doors, as outlined in the chapter by Patel and Pearce. As the chapters from

Leeds, Sheffield and London remind us, the younger the child, the less visible they are likely to be on the streets. This therefore requires vigilance on the part of those agencies tasked with caring for these young people and/or enforcing the law against those who exploit them.

The Act also covers the activity of 'causing or encouraging a child into commercial sexual exploitation; facilitating the commercial sexual exploitation of a child and controlling the activities of a child involved in prostitution or pornography'. The maximum penalty for all these crimes will be 14 years imprisonment (Home Office, 2002: 30). The chapters from Sheffield, Nottingham and Wolverhampton inform us that in the past they have had to resort to legislation such as the Child Abduction Act (1984) in order to pursue prosecutions against men involved in exploiting these young people. The new legislation hopefully means that this will no longer be necessary.

We would also expect that this new legislation will facilitate investigation and prosecution of those men involved in controlling young people through violence, sexual assault and/or rape – even when the young women concerned consider these men to be their 'boyfriends' as detailed in contributions from London and Bristol. Cases such as those described in the contributions from Nottingham and Wolverhampton, where, respectively, one adult was found to be 'controlling' five boys and another was linked to 15 young people involved in prostitution, will hopefully become a thing of the past.

Many of the contributions to this volume testify to the fact that it is often difficult for young women to complain about their treatment at the hands of abusive or controlling men. On the one hand, as Patel and Pearce show, this is often a result of 'intense emotional attachments' or, on the other hand as a result of fear of violent retribution as discussed in the chapter by Lucas and colleagues. The contributions from Nottingham and Wolverhampton show us that it has been possible in the past to bring prosecutions against such men without the young person necessarily being required to give evidence in court. It is to be hoped that the new legislation will make such prosecutions easier to achieve and will not require the young person to give evidence.

The Act recognises for the first time that paying for the sexual services of a child or young person constitutes 'child abuse' and renders the adult 'punter' culpable for the offence. This should mean, for young people like those discussed in this book, that they will no longer face the prospect of criminalisation as a result of their involvement in commercial sexual exploitation, and that their risk of sexual exploitation by abusive adults will, as a result, be reduced. Hopefully, the new legislation will give new impetus to the 'paradigm shift' set in train by the DoH guidance of 2000 (Melrose and Ayre, 2000; Ayre and Barrett, 2000; Barrett and Melrose, 2003). However, contributions such as that from Leeds, demonstrate that amongst statutory services there is a need to formalise procedures and to ensure that all statutory services take responsibility for this issue. We may then hope that some real change may be effected in terms of harmonising responses to and treatment of these young people.

In theory, the new legislation should make the work of practitioners, much easier in terms of pursuing and prosecuting those who sexually exploit young people. As the chapter from Sheffield concludes, work with young women to move them out of prostitution cannot be effective unless measures are in place to tackle the men who 'buy' their services or the men who take advantage of their vulnerabilities to exploit and control them.

In practice, it will be interesting to see whether, how robustly, and to what extent, the new legislation will be enforced and how it might sit with earlier government guidance in relation to the treatment of, and responses to young people involved in prostitution (DoH/HO/DfEE, 2000). For example, will the new legislation override the concept of 'persistently and voluntarily' returning to prostitution, contained in the earlier guidelines? Will it mean that no police officer can ever again regard young people involved in commercial sexual exploitation as just a 'hazard of the job' as the contribution from Leeds informs us they do? We hope so.

Having legislation on the statute books is no guarantee that it will change attitudes or be acted on in practice in the ways we might wish. Since kerb crawling became an offence in 2000, for example, a glance at the statistics shows that women involved in prostitution are still much more likely to be criminalised for their activities than are the men who seek to pay for their services. This appears to be a consequence of both pragmatism and attitudes since it is easier, and requires fewer resources, to secure convictions against the women involved than the men and, perhaps because the activities of the men involved may be tacitly condoned by those whose job it is to enforce the legislation.

Since the dissolution of the former Soviet Union with the consequent political reconfiguration of Europe, trafficking in people, especially women and children for the purpose of sexual exploitation, has become a much more prevalent problem in countries both within and outside Europe (IPES, 2004; Melrose et al., 2004). In this context, the Sexual Offences Act 2003 is very welcome. Under this legislation the offence of trafficking covers:

> . . . *recruiting, harbouring and facilitating the movement of another person for the purpose of commercial sexual exploitation . . . It will apply to persons trafficked from one place to another within the UK as well as across international borders.*

(Home Office, 2002: 31).

Concrete evidence of this crime is hard to come by for several reasons. Firstly, as a result of the paucity of official data on such trafficking in many countries this remains a largely 'hidden' problem involving an almost 'invisible' population (Lehti, 2003). Secondly, as a result of its connections with organised criminal networks, this activity is not amenable to the usual data gathering techniques (Kelly and Regan, 2000). Thirdly, because this traffic involves huge amounts of money, those charged with enforcing the law in some of these countries could be tempted to accept bribes from traffickers to ignore this trade. Fourthly, because many of the women and children involved are subject to threats of violence towards themselves or their families, they may be unwilling to complain to the authorities.

The most authoritative study to date records that 71 cases of women being trafficked in the UK were known to the police but suggests that somewhere between 142 and 1420 women and children are trafficked into the UK annually for the purpose of commercial sexual exploitation. The authors are clear, however, that the numbers are very hard to verify with any degree of accuracy and that the real figures may be ten or twenty times greater than those which are actually recorded (Kelly and Regan, 2000). A Home Office pilot project, established in London in February 2003, to support the victims of trafficking networks had, by May 2004, received 120 referrals and was housing 35 women – its maximum capacity (Taylor, 2004). These figures demonstrate that the demand for services from victims of trafficking networks is currently much greater than those that are available. To our knowledge, this is the only 'safe house' that currently exists in the UK for adult women who are victims of trafficking networks. Nationally, we are aware of only one such safe house for children and young people.

The offence of trafficking in people for the purpose of sexual exploitation was explicitly defined as a crime in the Nationality, Immigration and Asylum Act 2002. This offence was revisited in the Sexual Offences Act 2003, which devotes a whole section to this offence. Section 57 criminalises trafficking *into* the UK for this purpose; section 58 criminalises trafficking *within* the UK and section 59 criminalises trafficking *from* the UK. The maximum penalty for these offences is 14 years imprisonment (Home Office, 2002: 31).

The new legislation against trafficking in people for the purpose of commercial sexual exploitation is important in recognising that trafficking networks may operate *within* national boundaries as well as across them. This is important in the context of the commercial sexual exploitation of young people like those who are the subject of this book. It should mean that, in theory, it will no longer be possible for young women and men to be moved to different parts of the country or for them to 'disappear' from one area only to reappear in another. The contributors to this volume describe such instances. Foley and colleagues, for example, refer to cases of young women 'vanishing' from Bristol. The contribution from Nottingham talks of young men being trafficked to London in order to make pornographic videos.

The chapter by Lucas and colleagues suggests that young women are sometimes taken to work in other cities while Duffin's chapter provides evidence that young women are removed from his area to work in saunas in London. The new legislation will hopefully allow as much attention to be paid to these practices as to those which involve crossing international borders.

It is the hope of the editors of this volume that this new legislation will make a real difference to the lives of young people involved in commercial sexual exploitation and further facilitate the practice of those working with them. We would hope that if we were to revisit these practitioners a year from now, they would be able to report that it had.

CHAPTER 1

Of Tricks and Other Things: An Overview

Margaret Melrose

Introduction

This book is something of a double-edged sword. On the one hand, it represents an exciting opportunity for us to learn from each other and symbolises a massive step forward in terms of practice with children and young people involved in commercial sexual exploitation. On the other hand, however, it prompts deeply disturbing questions about the position of disadvantaged and vulnerable young people in Britain today. The fact that we now have different models of working with young people in different areas of the country to draw on, positively demonstrates the extent to which awareness of this issue has advanced in a relatively short period of time (see e.g. Barrett, 1997; Melrose, 2001). Nevertheless, the fact that there is a need to produce a book such as this is a sorry indictment of the state of 'childhood' and 'youth' for many children and young people in Britain today. Throughout this work, we employ a definition of 'children' and 'young people' as legally constituted by the Children Act 1989 – that is, anyone up to the age of 18. For this reason, the terms 'children' and 'young people' are used interchangeably throughout the text.

Awareness of the issue of young people exploited through prostitution has been raised in recent years primarily as a result of work undertaken by major children's charities (see Lee and O'Brien, 1995; Barrett, 1997; Barnardo's, 1998; Melrose et al., 1999). An increased awareness of the issue amongst a variety of statutory agencies, voluntary sector organisations and professional groups has resulted in the introduction of new government guidance in relation to the treatment of, and response to, young people who are abused through prostitution (DoH/HO/DfEE, 2000). This demonstrates the extent to which the problem has moved up the political agenda and represents a major advance in so far as there is now at least an official recognition that such a problem exists in Britain after many years of official denial (Brown and Barrett, 2002).

Although locally, nationally (and internationally) the scale of this problem remains unknown (McNeish, 1998), we now know a lot more than we previously did about young people who are involved in commercial sexual exploitation in Britain. In their literature review in Chapter 3, Drinkwater and

Greenwood provide a brief overview of what we know to date. We know, for example, from the contributions in this book that the extent of the problem is much more widespread than may previously have been imagined (see also, Brain et al., 1998; Melrose et al., 1999). We also know, and the various contributors to this volume certify, that this problem exists in many towns and cities across the UK and is not just confined to major metropolitan or urban areas (see Brain et al., 1998; Melrose et al., 1999). In addition, we know that young men as well as young women are involved (Barrett, 1997). What we know of their involvement, and that of young women, is discussed in Chapter 3 by Drinkwater and Greenwood. In Chapter 8 Tim Darch makes a significant contribution by describing methods of working with young men. This model stands alone in this volume, however, many of the contributors demonstrate that they are becoming increasingly aware of this issue as it relates to young men and it is to be hoped that there will be more of such models to draw on in future.

As a result of contributions to this volume and other empirically based research (for example, Barnardos, 1998; Melrose et al., 1999; Phoenix, 2001) we are beginning to understand more about the aetiology of the problem, the methods through which young people become involved and the sorts of things that serve to ensnare them once they are involved (Melrose et al., 1999). As a result, we are also more aware of what needs to be done in practice in order to respond effectively to these young people and at the same time we are more aware of what should *not* be done (Melrose, 2001). The examples of good practice presented in this volume serve further to underline and emphasise examples of inadequate or inappropriate responses to these young people.

The professionals who have contributed to this book demonstrate how to work with these young people in order to provide examples and guidance for other practitioners involved in this challenging area of work. They come from a range of professional backgrounds in voluntary and statutory sector organisations, for example, social work, youth work, and the police and all discuss what has worked for them and the young people with whom they are concerned in this complex and challenging area of work. There are also academic contributions in the form of a discussion of historical constructions of young people involved in prostitution in Chapter 2, a literature review in Chapter 3 and a model of action research in Chapter 7.

It is important that we acknowledge the valour of the contributors for agreeing to write their chapters and of their senior managers for allowing them to make this contribution. It is after all easier to say 'no' when asked to produce a piece of work for a book of this kind because no one wants the area in which they live and work associated with the child sex trade. We therefore recognise and applaud such courage and gratefully acknowledge the contribution of each of the authors.

Where are the child prostitutes then?

We have thought long and hard about issues of identification and anonymity in relation to the sites that these contributions have come from. We want to promote good practice and one means of doing that is to show what other projects are doing. We also of course want the good work that all these projects are engaged in acknowledged. We have considered that, for this reason, the projects themselves may not want to be anonymous. However, we also want to protect children and consider that the best way to do that is not to draw unwarranted and unwanted attention to those areas where young people are at risk of, or involved in, commercial sexual exploitation. We have therefore attempted, as far as has been possible, to anonymise the precise localities from which contributors are speaking while leaving the cities and towns from which they have come identifiable. We realise that not everyone will be happy with this decision but we considered it the best line to tread so that the contributions are not overly depersonalised nor the situations in which they are working de-contextualised or denied.

Joined-up working

In line with government guidance, all contributors affirm the importance of developing multi-agency and inter-disciplinary approaches to respond appropriately to the needs of young people involved in commercial sexual exploitation. In addition, they testify to the importance of having agreed protocols and procedures in place to tackle the problem and to ensure that these young people are protected from further abuse. The contributions in this book attest to the importance of keeping the welfare of the young people in sight at all times and in everything that is done to respond to them. They remind us that the issue of young people who are exploited through prostitution is multi-faceted and profoundly complex and therefore beyond the scope of a single agency to respond to effectively. Achieving such a 'joined-up' response in practice, however, may be rather more difficult than it sounds and in order to do so, a number of complexities and challenges need to be confronted and overcome if the young people, and the practitioners concerned, are to reap the rewards of partnership work.

First, and foremost, agencies working together need to build relationships of trust if they are to work effectively in partnership (Crawford, 1997 cited in Crawford, 1998). It is important to recognise that this may take some time when agencies with different value bases and goals seek to establish a common ground. Once established, it is essential to acknowledge the 'fragility' of trust relationships and therefore their need for 'on-going nurturing and monitoring' (Crawford, 1998). The need to ensure a confidential service for the young people on one hand with the need to share information about them with other practitioners on the other, for instance, is a matter of delicate negotiation in partnership arrangements and is an issue around which conflicts and tensions may arise (see Chapter 7 and Chapter 10 of this volume). Additionally, or alternatively, conflicts may arise between 'harm minimisation' and 'child protection' approaches to the work (see Chapter 8 in this volume).

There are of course different models of partnership working that represent 'ideal types'. On the one hand, there is a model of 'inter-agency' working while on the other, a model of 'multi-agency' working (Crawford and Jones, 1996 cited in Crawford, 1998:174). In the former there is some degree of loss of organisational autonomy for the agencies involved because this type of partnership arrangement requires some amount of 'fusion and melding' between the agencies involved (Crawford, 1998:175). In multi-agency working, agencies come together without it affecting significantly the work they do within their own organisations. 'The same tasks are conducted in co-operation with others' but the role of various partners remains distinct (Crawford, 1998:174). When key representatives of agencies or institutions come together in multi-agency work, 'core tasks remain unaltered as multi-agency work is grafted on to existing practices or those existing practices are redefined' (Crawford, 1998:175). Chapters 4 and 5 demonstrate how they have developed effective multi-agency responses to the problem of young people exploited through prostitution.

In the real world of course, actual partnership working will probably fall somewhere between these two 'ideal types'. The contributors to this book demonstrate that successful partnership arrangements have been established either between statutory agencies and/or statutory agencies and voluntary sector organisations together to ensure the best interests of the children concerned. These models of partnership working allow for a holistic approach to the issue of children abused through prostitution that is 'problem focused rather than bureaucratically driven' (Crawford, 1998). At the same time, they provide new possibilities for generating creative responses to meet the needs of the young people concerned. This is demonstrated in Chapter 7 by Patel and Pearce who draw on their experience of working with an innovative project run by the NSPCC to show the positive outcomes of thinking in new ways to develop, for example, 'therapeutic outreach'.

Many of the chapters also demonstrate that partnership working promotes tolerance and better understanding between practitioners from different professional backgrounds. Additionally, working in partnerships enables pre-existing barriers between organisational cultures to be broken down. It is important to accept, therefore, that there are *both* challenges *and* rewards in partnership working.

Some observations on terminology

The guidance introduced by the New Labour government in relation to the treatment of and response to young people involved in prostitution (DoH/HO/DfEE, 2000) has effected something of a paradigm shift in how young people involved in prostitution are defined in official discourse and responded to by official agencies. This is represented in practice as a shift from a 'punishment' to a 'welfare' model (Ayre and Barrett, 2000). As a result, there has been a concomitant shift in the language we employ to define and talk about these young people (Melrose, 2002). Previously, euphemisms such as 'young sex worker' were employed by those working in the field who were concerned to minimise the stigma that attaches to those, young and old, involved in prostitution. Although these heretofore employed terms were kindly meant, Pitts (1997) has pointed out that, in fact, they served merely to conceal 'the enormity of the violation to which these young people were subject'. It is now widely accepted that young people's involvement in prostitution does not result from a 'free economic or moral choice' (DoH/HO/DfEE, 2000). It has therefore become more common to refer to them as 'young people involved in commercial sexual exploitation' (see Patel and Pearce this volume, Pearce, 2000a; 2000b) or as 'young people abused through prostitution' (see Barnardo's, 1998). In this volume therefore, the terms 'young people involved in commercial sexual exploitation', 'young people abused through prostitution' and 'young people involved in prostitution' are used interchangeably.

Talking of children and young people involved in prostitution has become something of a semantic minefield. While the politics of language may appear to be a rather esoteric discussion to have in the context of a book that is intended for practitioners, language and our interpretations of social reality are not disconnected. The terminology we employ is an extremely important component of how the issue is constructed, understood and responded to in practice. All contributors to this volume demonstrate their sensitivity to this issue.

The issue of how we define young people's involvement in commercial sexual exploitation is extremely important because, depending on how we define the problem we will produce different estimates of its scale (Lee, 1993) and develop different responses in practice. The time has perhaps come to begin to distinguish between what might be termed 'thick' and 'thin' definitions. By this, we mean that it is necessary to recognise that in the past 20 years or so, the sex industry has expanded and diversified enormously (see for example, Scambler and Scambler, 1997; Weitzer, 2000). As a result of new technology (the internet, mobile phones, commercial tourism and so on) there has been a proliferation of telephone sex lines, an increase in the availability of pornography and a growth in prostitution in both on and off street locations. In short, there has been a prolific increase in the potential for young people to become involved in commercial sexual exploitation and a multiplication of the sites through which, or at which, they may do so (Melrose and Brown, 2002). We would argue, therefore, in line with the present government, that there is a need to employ a 'thick' definition of commercial sexual exploitation and to recognise, as Gregory and Winton do in Chapter 4 that the term 'commercial sexual exploitation' can include:

The prostitution of children and young people; the production, sale, marketing and possession of pornographic material involving children; the distribution of pornographic pictures of children over the internet; trafficking in children; and sex tourism involving children.

(DoH/HO, 2001).

All the contributors to this volume discuss young people's involvement in 'prostitution' (selling or 'swapping' sexual 'favours' for some form of reward). They recognise, however, as Gregory and Winton in Chapter 4 and Foley and colleagues in Chapter 9 demonstrate, that their involvement in prostitution renders them vulnerable to other forms of predation and other forms of exploitation within the contemporary sex industry. Young people may be involved in commercial sexual exploitation in a variety of locations (on or off street, for example) and under various terms and conditions (O'Connell-Davidson, 1998 and see Chapters 7 and 10 in this volume). A young person may 'self-prostitute', for example, or another may force them into prostitution. This is discussed more fully in Chapter 3 by Drinkwater and Greenwood, in Chapter 10 by Wilkinson-Shaw and later in this chapter when we consider the means by which young people become involved in commercial sexual exploitation.

Because the language has become highly significant – but loaded, cumbersome and perhaps not expressive enough of the material conditions these young people encounter, some contributors, such as Lucas and colleagues in Chapter 5, have attempted to refine definitions of young people involved in 'commercial sexual exploitation'. They have attempted to distinguish between those believed to be 'at risk' of involvement and those already involved. The former are said to be involved in 'sexual exploitation' (for example in relationships with older men) while the latter are involved in '*commercial* sexual exploitation' (prostitution). In Chapter 7, Patel and Pearce also point to the importance of the language and terminology we employ to talk about these young people. They argue that as girls under 16 cannot consent to sex, they cannot be associated actively with activities related to prostitution and therefore should not be referred to as 'prostitutes'.

The context of commercial sexual exploitation of young people

The issue of children abused through prostitution cannot be understood outside of the political, historical, economic and social conditions that give rise to this phenomenon (O'Neill, 2001). The profound social, economic and political changes that have occurred in Britain in the past 20-25 years, labour market reorganisation and welfare retrenchment, for example, have inadvertently created the conditions in which the commercial sexual exploitation of children and young people has been able to flourish (Melrose et al., 1999; Melrose, 2000b; Melrose and Barrett, 2001; Melrose and Ayre, 2002). It has recently been argued, for example, that 'Europe today is characterised by the free movement of goods and girls' (Duval, 1996 cited in Fekete and Webber, 1997).

The sex industry has grown exponentially in Britain and the rest of the world in this period (Weitzer, 2000). We have witnessed what might be described as the sexualisation of global relations and the globalisation of sexual relations (see for example Weeks, 2002). Encapsulated within this 'growth industry' is a burgeoning market in children (Brown, 2000; Melrose and Brown, 2002). In some cases this may simply be because 'men like fresh meat' (see Melrose et al., 1999), in others it may be because young people are assumed to be free of sexually transmitted diseases (STDs) as a result of their young ages. It has even been suggested that in some countries a belief abounds that having sex with a pre-pubescent girl is a 'cure' for AIDS (Brown, 2000).

As many chapters in this volume demonstrate, those men who are involved in the commercial sexual abuse of children, whether by paying for their 'services' or by forcing them into prostitution, are frequently involved in other serious crimes such as drug dealing or possession of firearms. They are often ruthless and very dangerous men indeed. Gregory and Winton, Chapter 4, Lucas and colleagues, Chapter 5, Duffin, Chapter 6, and Foley and colleagues in Chapter 9 echo this insight. They show that young women are at extreme risk from violent and dangerous adults (mostly men) and as a consequence, the streets are becoming an increasingly dangerous place for vulnerable young people. These contributors therefore emphasise the importance of targeting abusive adults *at the same time* as undertaking work to support and protect the young people.

Becoming involved in prostitution

All the contributions in this volume bear witness to the fact that young people become involved in commercial sexual exploitation for a range of complex and inter-connected – even overlapping – reasons and that it is seldom possible to pinpoint a single 'cause'. Rather, there is a complex interaction between a range of 'push' and 'pull' factors and between individual and environmental factors. Chapter 3 by Drinkwater and Greenwood provides a fuller discussion of this issue. Many of the contributors, for example, Lucas and colleagues in Chapter 5, Patel and Pearce in Chapter 7, Darch in Chapter 8, Foley and colleagues in Chapter 9 and Wilkinson-Shaw in Chapter 10 demonstrate that drugs are an increasingly important factor in young people being abused through prostitution. This may be because they have developed a drug habit – especially in relation to the use of heroin or crack cocaine – and then become involved in commercial sexual activity in order to fund their drug use. Alternatively, it may be that abusive adults provide them with drugs with the intention of luring them into sex work. However their drug problems start or develop, it is clear that drug use is a major complicating factor in trying to work with these young people and it is necessary to make provisions for responding to this level of need when planning service responses for these young people (Melrose, 2000a).

How young people become involved in commercial sexual exploitation remains a matter of some controversy. Although the debate is complex, it can be simplistically characterised as those adhering to a 'pimping and grooming' model (Barnardo's, 1998) on the one side and those who argue, on the other side, that young people can and do make decisions for themselves and that sometimes these decisions involve them in becoming involved in prostitution. The former tend to argue that young people involved in prostitution are the victims of abusive adults who have coerced them into prostitution. Many of the contributors to this volume appear to subscribe to this model. On the other hand, Drinkwater and Greenwood in Chapter 3 show in their literature review that peer group influences and clusters can be an important part of understanding young people's entry to, and sustained involvement in, prostitution. In Chapter 10, Wilkinson-Shaw acknowledges that sometimes, young people themselves make the decision to prostitute although she does not dispute that such a decision usually results from severely constrained options or highly structured choices (Pitts, 1997; Pettiway, 1997).

This debate is not helped by the fact that there is little empirical evidence to support one side or the other and what evidence does exist is drawn primarily from small scale, local agency studies (but see Melrose et al., 1999 for an exception). It is of course possible that there are regional variations in the organisation and operation of child sex markets and what might be true of one area will not necessarily be true of another. Politically, this debate is extremely sensitive since if we are arguing that these young people should be treated as victims of abuse, then there are certain vested interests in showing that they are involved in prostitution as a result of being coerced by an abusive adult rather than as a result of their own agency. Brown picks up this point in Chapter 2. Her chapter traces 'childhood' as a discursive construction and demonstrates that historically, young people involved in prostitution have been represented either as 'culpable villains' or as 'abused and helpless victims'. Brown's chapter also shows that the model of 'pimping and grooming' derives predominately from a discourse of childhood, which originates in the nineteenth century, and through which young people (particularly young women) are defined as innocent, asexual, vulnerable or helpless. This discourse, as Brown demonstrates, is particularly associated with the work of the National Vigilance Society of the 1890s.

While this model is important in identifying that becoming involved in prostitution is a social *process*, it appears not to acknowledge that this process occurs within particular historical, economic, political, ideological, social and even technological conditions. It is therefore equally important to acknowledge that this model does not necessarily tell the whole story and that it is limited because it tends to deny the agency of the young people themselves (see Melrose et al., 1999). As we have seen above, sex markets are dynamic and constantly changing – they are not trans-historical or trans-spatial. What may explain a young person's involvement in one time and place will not necessarily explain the involvement of a different young person in another time and place. As these markets develop, expand, and become more sophisticated, so too must our understandings of them if we are to effect appropriate interventions.

Questions about *how* and *why* young people become involved in commercial sexual exploitation are extremely important for practice because it is evident that different reasons for becoming involved will require different responses to effect exit (see Melrose, 2000a). If a young person is involved because an abusive adult has coerced them, then it is obviously crucial that every attempt is made to disrupt that abusive relationship. If, on the other hand, a young person is involved because they regard prostitution as a viable source of income, then alternative interventions and responses need to be sought. In short, the reason for the young person's involvement must be determined in order to develop an effective response.

Acknowledging that there are some young people involved in prostitution who have *not* been forced into it by an abusive adult may seem like political suicide to those who have campaigned long and hard to have these children and young people accepted as in need of care and protection rather than punishment. However, this need not necessarily be so. This acknowledgement demands that we consider the circumstances in which the decision to prostitute appears as a viable option. It forces us to recognise that for many of these young people 'the relationships and networks that ordinarily might have prevented their drift into self-destructive or self-defeating behaviour are absent' (Pitts, 1997:149). This recognition compels us to acknowledge that prostitution only appears as a viable option for those young people whose past experiences and present circumstances are so negative and reduced that they feel there is no alternative (Pitts, 1997). It is precisely these young people who are most in need of care and protection (Melrose and Barrett, 1999).

What do young people abused through prostitution need?

All the contributions in this book testify to the fact that young people involved in commercial sexual exploitation are usually desperately vulnerable and socially isolated in the sense that they are often lacking appropriate support systems and positive helping networks. They demonstrate that the young people are often struggling with issues of self-esteem and self-worth and need support and encouragement from practitioners in order to be able to value themselves. In order to receive the support they need, the young people require a comprehensive range of 'joined-up' services to meet a range of complex needs (Melrose, 2001), as all the chapters demonstrate. The chapters by Patel and Pearce, Darch, Foley and colleagues and Wilkinson-Shaw show that these services need to be available outside of normal office hours. It is clear that in order to attract the resources required to provide these services, the issue of commercial sexual exploitation of young people needs to be 'mainstreamed' through other services. This might be achieved, for example, by incorporating these issues into the educational curriculum (through PHSE), through youth service provision (Connexions) or through incorporating the issue into local Crime and Disorder Strategies.

All the contributors also show that young people involved in commercial sexual exploitation can sometimes be 'hard to reach' and difficult to engage. This may be the case especially when the young person is in a 'relationship' with an abusive adult ('pimp') or when they have established substance misuse problems. Additionally, as the contributors demonstrate, they are likely to be suspicious of 'helping' agencies and 'authority figures' because they often perceive that they have been, at best, let down by adults and, at worst, abused by them in the past. In this respect, the importance of persisting in trying to engage the young person cannot be overstated. There is therefore a need for practitioners to be patient and to offer a non-judgemental and non-discriminatory ear and hand and for the child to know that they are 'there for them' (Melrose, 2001). In this way, trust between the child and the practitioner may be established, and in time this may provide an opportunity to undertake work with them that may eventually enable them to exit from prostitution. It is important for practitioners to be cognisant of the fact, as those who have contributed to this volume have acknowledged, that this is likely to be a long haul. There is a need to accept that there are no magic wands to wave or overnight solutions in this field of practice.

What do practitioners need?

We hope that practitioners will feel they need this book and that it will help them to reflect on and develop their own practice in this field. It is also clear that practitioners need the resources to respond to the levels of need that they encounter in their work. At this point in time, we have sadly to acknowledge that such resources are not always available. The contributors to this volume, for example, identify, in particular, a level of unmet need for appropriate housing and drug treatment services for young people. Until such resources are forthcoming, practitioners will always be, to some extent, struggling against the tide in this area of work.

It also behoves us to acknowledge at this point that this is an extremely demanding, and often highly stressful, area of work for those involved in it. It is not always possible to leave such work 'at the door' and practitioners themselves may therefore be in need of support from within their organisations (Melrose, 2002). This point is well made in Chapter 7 by Patel and Pearce, who in their work, recognised and made provision for front-line workers to receive regular and appropriate support. Adopting this model is something that practitioners in other regions and organisations might usefully consider.

Organisation of the chapters

There is a clear overlap between the themes addressed in the different chapters of this book for which we make no apology. This simply demonstrates that many practitioners, in different areas of the country, are facing very similar types of challenges and grappling with the same sorts of complexities in working with young people involved in commercial sexual exploitation. They have all, however, devised effective ways of working in partnership to deliver the services these young people so desperately need.

The book begins with academic perspectives in Chapters 2 and 3. Chapter 2 looks historically at the ways in which 'child prostitutes' have been discursively constructed in England since the nineteenth century and throughout the twentieth. Chapter 3 then provides a review of what we know to date about this issue in Britain in the form of a literature review. Chapters 4 and 5 discuss how to build effective partnerships to respond to this problem based on their respective experiences in Nottinghamshire and Sheffield. In Chapter 4, a joint social services and police perspective is presented and in Chapter 5, a view from Sheffield ACPC sexual exploitation project developed with Home Office funding. Chapter 6 provides a viewpoint from the police and discusses how the experience of the ACPO pilot in Wolverhampton (Brain et al., 1998) led to a transformation in the police response to this issue.

Subsequently, the book provides readers with views from different voluntary sector agencies. Chapter 7 provides an action research model developed jointly through the work of the NSPCC and Middlesex University to respond to young women involved in commercial sexual exploitation. The authors suggest that this model is equally applicable to work with young men. Chapters 8 and 9 reflect on their experience of working in a multi-agency partnership to respond to the needs of young people in Bristol. Chapter 8 provides a model for working with young men and Chapter 9 a model for working with young women. Chapter 10 discusses the standpoint of a voluntary sector service that was originally developed to meet the needs of adult women but which has since expanded its provision to meet the needs of girls and young women. The concluding chapter looks at how far we have come in terms of understanding and responding to this issue in recent years, where we are now and where we still need to go. It also considers future challenges in this difficult area of work and makes recommendations for future policy and practice.

Finally, we hope that by sharing their experiences, the contributors to this volume will appreciate the very positive contribution they have made to this developing field of practice. It may feel like a very small step forward but, in our estimation, it represents a huge advance. Ultimately, however, that is for our readers to judge.

CHAPTER 2

Historical Constructions of Child Prostitution in England

Alyson Brown

Introduction

This chapter examines constructions of child prostitution during the twentieth century, the origins of these representations and the extent to which these images of 'the child prostitute' have been used as a metaphor for other perceived social, economic and political problems. During the twentieth century, children who have been sexually abused through prostitution have often been lost in the interstices between discourses that portray them as either abducted and coerced innocents, or as assertive and blameworthy seducers.

The twentieth century has been referred to as the century of the child, the historical period in which the concept of childhood was clarified and elucidated in law, labour markets, education and the medical arena as well as in other contexts. If the idea of childhood as distinct and requiring particular accommodation and restraint was established by the end of the nineteenth century, then childhood has been examined, elaborated and provided for during the twentieth century as never before. However, the avoidance of some issues regarding children has been particularly evident when the taboo subjects of sex and sexuality have been involved, so that child prostitution and child sexual abuse remained issues largely debated in criminal justice, medical or social welfare circles.

One consequence of this is that the meaning of 'child prostitution', and the characteristics of children involved in underage commercial sexual activity, have been abstracted from negatives. Children involved in prostitution have therefore been perceived as *not* asexual, dependent, moral or 'real' children, but also *not* as adults. This tendency for negative abstraction has meant that children involved in prostitution have been seen as sexually assertive, independent, immoral, and as a distorted or perverse form of childhood. Hence, over the last century, as discourses of child sexual abuse were being constructed, those relating to child prostitution have taken a distinct journey, one more likely to lead to condemnation and even criminalisation.

This distinction has only been seriously challenged during the 1980s and 1990s when the involvement of children in commercial sex attracted significant government and public attention. Thus, as one writer has noted, 'Within the field of child welfare, the emergence of new areas of need is more often than not the rediscovery of some very old ones' (Van Meeuwen, 1998: 3). This is one of the reasons why the term 'prostitute' is used here to refer to children in the sex trade. It is not to suggest that they should be considered as something other than as victims of sexual abuse, indeed sexual abuse through prostitution is precisely what these children experience. It is rather because the term 'child prostitution' was used by historical contemporaries and thus should be considered in that light. Because of its long usage, the term informs the nature of the activity involved in a way that no other term allows. Certainly, the continued use of euphemisms and the obscuring of the abusive exploitation by punters and pimps have played a part in the continuing attribution of blame to the underage victim of this form of sexual abuse – the child prostitute.

Constructing the threatening child

The historical use of language, such as 'moral danger' and 'corruption' in relation to the sexual behaviour and/or vulnerability of children has, in one respect, served to summon up the worst of images. Such terminology has exacerbated the stigmatisation of girls with 'knowledge of evil' (Brown and Barrett, 2002). Along with the continued sensitivity of such subjects, this has increased problems regarding the detection and prosecution of cases of child sexual abuse and of the exploitation of children through prostitution.

The perceived dangerousness of child sexuality is a theme that has been highlighted by other writers and is evident in Hendrick's (1994: 1–2) discussion of the dualism inherent in the portrayal of children as both victims and threats. Children involved in prostitution have been epitomised as 'dangerous' because they have not conformed to idealised versions of childhood or to popular, and largely fictional, images of a 'white slave trade' in which pure and innocent victims were abducted, drugged and forced to work in brothels overseas.

Historical constructions of child prostitution have also been influenced by associations which have varied in particular social, political and economic contexts, for example, with regard to the ideologies of childhood and the family; the perceived threat of lower class social standards; links made to the criminal underworld and so forth. This has also been identified by Doezema, who notes that:

> While the discourse on white slavery ostensibly was about the protection of women from (male) violence, to a large extent, the welfare of the 'white slaves' was peripheral to the discourse. A supposed threat to women's safety served as a marker of and metaphor for other fears, among them fear of women's growing independence, the breakdown of the family, and loss of national identity through the influx of immigrants.
>
> (Doezema, 1999: 17).

An important factor is the malleability of such a 'dangerous' and shocking image as that of child prostitution. It is this that has provided additional impact when it has been related to various identified social problems. The difficulty has often been attempting to decipher the actuality behind the rhetoric.

Historical constructions of child prostitution and the malleability of the term have mitigated against the conceptualisation of child prostitution as a form of sexual abuse. Negative portrayals of child prostitutes as sexually knowledgeable, and the assumption of choice on the part of the child, have been instrumental in excluding child prostitution from definitions of child sexual abuse.

Alongside images of dangerousness, historically there has been a reluctance to accept the involvement of children in commercial sex. This has encouraged an image of such children as abducted and betrayed innocents. The mid-to-late nineteenth century was a formative period in the construction of these images and representations of child prostitution for the next century or more. Attention to this issue was fuelled by a now well-known series of sensationalist articles written and published by W. T.Stead in the *Pall Mall Gazette* (6,7,8,10 and 22 July 1885). These 'Maiden Tribute' articles provided the crucial force to ensure the final passage of the Criminal Law Amendment Act 1885, which increased the age of consent from 13 to 16 years of age and augmented police powers to deal with vice. The balance between control or protection then became an enduring feature of debates on child prostitution.

During the late nineteenth century, the power of the depiction of pure and innocent child victims *versus* their brutal and predatory abusers became the cause which united feminists, social purity organisations and religious bodies to campaign for an increase in the age of consent and other child protection measures. They served effectively to highlight the sexual and physical abuse of both women and children by men and to bring about the 'purification of national life' (Mort, 1987). Indeed, the cultural myth of the white slave trade partly operated to redirect condemnation from the 'victim' to the exploiter and from women to men by constructing an image of the victim of sexual abuse requiring unquestioned protection (Irwin, 1996: 3). The term 'white slave' was in common usage by the 1870s and became the parody which denoted the abduction and violation of innocent youth by, usually foreign, evil agents, thus incorporating concerns about overseas threats to British Imperialism. It also operated to obscure the rationales that led young girls into commercial sex, the nature of their abuse and the personal consequences for them.

Deborah Gorham and Judith Walkowitz believe that in late Victorian Britain many underage girls were engaged in prostitution, but through economic necessity 'because their choices were so limited', and not as the 'passive, sexually innocent victims' depicted by Stead (Gorham, 1978: 355; Walkowitz,

1992). Louise Jackson takes a more nuanced approach, suggesting that many accounts of juvenile prostitution were themselves euphemistic descriptions of child sexual abuse that allowed the problem to be more acceptably articulated by locating it outside of the home and family (2000: 16). To an extent, this may have been the case, and Jackson effectively highlights the problems of interpretation as a result of the evasive language often used in relation to sexual issues at the time. However, since the term child prostitution represented a reasonably defined mode of behaviour, rather than more obscure or nebulous terms like 'corruption', it would also be appropriate to encompass an acceptance of the existence of child prostitution within the definition of child sexual abuse.

Constructing the 'normal' child

In late Victorian England, the rapid expansion of children's voluntary organisations sought to establish new standards for 'proper' child raising. This was illustrated in the Prevention of Cruelty to Children and Protection of Children Act 1889, which was extended and consolidated in 1894 and 1904. The NSPCC repeatedly claimed that its role was not to replace parental authority and responsibility but to reinforce it. In so doing they, and other children's societies, helped to distinguish between 'normal' and 'abnormal' family cultures which were considered to be productive of juvenile delinquency. One prominent theme in the rhetoric around juvenile delinquency constructed the vicious and sexually promiscuous girl, who, unless removed from her existing environment would drift inevitably into prostitution.

The strategy of the children's societies was to separate 'delinquents' from 'normal' children by associating them with concepts of dirt and filth, income earning and independence and in particular sexual knowledge (Mahood, 1995). The moral panic regarding child prostitution during this period was, as Jackson writes, 'part of a move to naturalise and normalise the childhood condition amongst all social classes' (2000: 17). Thus the concomitant middle class idealisation and sentimentalisation of children during the late nineteenth century and into the twentieth century has been described as 'sacralisation' (Zelizer in Hendrick, 1997: 10). Prominent in this were the removal of children from the economic sphere, and often from the environment/family which had allowed independence, and the shielding of them from sexual knowledge.

Social anxiety in late Victorian Britain centred upon representations of the children of the poor as either uncivilised, dangerous and precocious, morally and otherwise, or as revered innocents who required protection (Linehan, 1999). Child prostitutes tended to be constructed either as abducted innocents or as active participants in their sexual experience and therefore as blameworthy. Once the short step was made into being sexually knowing the child was tainted. It was not until the inter-war period that many feminist and child welfare organisations, including the NSPCC, consistently sought to 'explain sexual precociousness in young girls as an outcome of sexual abuse' (Smart, 1998: 12–3).

The Association for Moral and Social Hygiene (AMSH) and the National Vigilance Association (NVA) focused their strategies upon differing concerns. The former attempted to highlight the sexual activity or even promiscuity, and responsibility for such behaviour, of girls of 14 or 15, while the latter emphasised the sexual abuse of prepubescent children. The NVA concentrated their campaigning upon girls under ten years of age. Their reasoning was that there was a significant difference in offence between 'tampering with a child of seven or eight and premature sex relation with a girl nearing 16 with a young man of her acquaintance' (NVA Archive 4/BVA Box 199, 47th Annual Report, 1932: 11). Not only did this fail to address the issue of the sexuality of adolescent girls under 16 who could also be vulnerable, but it neatly side-stepped the issue of responsibility with regard to older girls.

In order to reduce sympathy for the abusers of older girls, particularly amongst the legal profession, the AMSH concentrated upon redefining these men as predatory rather than as being seduced. The AMSH highlighted the need for a balanced view of responsibilities and a realistic acceptance that with greater maturity should come greater blame not for the abused but for the abuser. Such debates within the AMSH paralleled important developments in the construction of child sexual abuse. These were reflected in legislation which restricted the defence of 'reasonable cause to believe that a girl was 16 years or over' to men aged 22 years or less (Criminal Law Amendment Act, 1922). Such concerns were also evident in the pressure that was brought to bear to modify court proceedings in sexual cases involving children and to increase penalties for sexual assault upon children.

Nevertheless, during the Commons debate on the Criminal Law Amendment Act of 1922 the depiction of the young, lower class girl as the sexually mature seducer of innocent young men was still evident. Indeed, one of a series of failed amendments to this Act sought to exclude girls who were prostitutes, and less than 16 years old, from legal protection. The image of the sexually assertive underage prostitute as bearing the responsibility as the seducer and as a threat to the sexual control of men persisted. Even the magistrates' periodical, the *Justice of the Peace* in 1925 depicted the underage subject of sexual assault as composing 'the helpless innocent child at the one end of the scale and the precocious temptress at the other' (2 January 1925).

Continued resistance to the idea that young people involved in prostitution were 'helpless innocent children' contributed to the weakening of campaigning pressures to address child sexual assault in all its forms. Sheila Jeffreys has suggested that during the inter-war period indignation against such assaults were dissipated in the face of responsibility increasingly being taken away from the male offender and attributed instead to exceptional psychological illness which framed the stereotypical abuser as both abnormal and as an outsider (1985: 152).

Yet the subject of children living in, or frequenting brothels was a significant factor in pre-Second World War child protection legislation (for example, The Children's Act of 1908 contained a measure to prevent children from frequenting 'the company of any common or reputed prostitute'). Inherent in this was a belief that prostitution was a lifetime or even a hereditary profession. Prostitution was regarded as at least irrevocably contaminating, and it was feared that prostitute mothers might introduce their own children to it. Certainly, there are examples of child prostitution from within the family to be found in the historical records of children's charities. A case in 1906 reported two under-nourished girls found living in a house which 'resembled a pigsty'. The elder girl, who was 15 years of age, was, according to the report 'being encouraged to earn her living by immorality'. Another case was revealed in 1913 in which a father had forced his 15 year old daughter under threats of violence, into prostitution and had been living on her earnings for at least a year (*Child's Guardian,* 1906 XX (7): 84 and 1913 XXVII (1): 4). Also, as part of an NSPCC investigation in the late 1920s in the South of England, witnesses testified to soldiers frequenting the house of their neighbour in the evenings. This household was headed by a woman with three children. Neighbours reported years of 'immoral' behaviour by the mother, and that the pregnancy of the daughter, who gave birth when only 14 years old, was 'the talk of the neighbours'.* On this occasion, and following at least one letter of complaint, the NSPCC spearheaded the move to investigate complaints from the local community, with the aid of the police once investigations had begun.

It was the NSPCC and the court that elicited and confirmed the moral standards of the individuals in the community who gave evidence. The local neighbourhood proved to be the arbiters in the constructions of the mother's reputation and behaviour. As Shani D'Cruze has noted with regard to violence against and by women during the nineteenth century, 'people occupied and moved across the grid of neighbourhood space under the regular observation of others. Although neighbours could prove a supportive

---

* Special permission to view this file was obtained from the NSPCC. Due to the sensitive nature of the subject all identifying references have been excluded.

and positive context for sociability, it could also be the crucible for innumerable tensions' (1998: 50–1).

Seductive children?

What is suggested by the examination of individual cases is that distinctions continued to be made between supposed child victims of abduction and those who became prostitutes through other less easily definable or understandable routes. Barry has suggested that even into the late twentieth century, part of the bias that has made the issue of forced prostitution invisible, originates in the concentration on how the girl gets into that position. She states that, if the girl is 'kidnapped, purchased, fraudulently contracted through an agency or organised crime, it is easy to recognise her victimisation. But if she enters slavery (prostitution) having been procured through love and befriending tactics, then few, including herself, are willing to recognise her victimisation' (Barry, 1979: 12).

Certainly, the important Street Offences Act of 1959 served to confirm the primacy placed upon the public face of prostitution rather than its possible role as a form of victimisation or of child sexual abuse. The term 'common prostitute' was retained, and no age distinction was made with reference to cautioning and conviction for soliciting. The High Court later (1994) confirmed that '*only* women can be charged with loitering under the Street Offences Act 1959' (Scambler and Scambler, 1997: 180). Only women, therefore, can be charged with offences that constitute 'prostitution'. Young men and boys are more likely to be charged under the Sexual Offences Act 1956 with offences such as 'obstructing the public highway' (Aitchison and O'Brien, 1997). Opposition to the Street Offences Bill in Parliament, however, did use the image of the underage prostitute plying her trade in public in an attempt to insert a clause that would have prohibited the conviction under this Act of any person below the age of 18. Leslie Hale, MP for Oldham West gave the image of:

> *The sort of bad girl who has got into trouble at home, quarrelled with her parents, committed a criminal offence and gone to an approved school. That is the background – and one knows the trouble that the approved schools have in dealing with these girls.*

> (Hansard, 5th series 22 April 1959, vol.604, col.446).

Distinctions that were made between child victims of abduction and those who became prostitutes through other less easily understandable routes became much more subject to critical examination during the 1980s and 1990s. In fact, while in her book, published in 1979, Kathleen Barry was asserting that this bias remained, she was also a part of this developing scrutiny. An important watershed in Britain came during the mid-1970s when the subject of child prostitution received widespread coverage in the national press for the first time since the late nineteenth century. Evidence that several underage girls may have been selling their bodies while in local authority care placed the unpleasant likelihood that many other children were doing the same indisputably before the public. The presentation of this evidence meant that child prostitution was much less open to being interpreted as an extraordinary or rare occurrence and indeed statements in the press from social work spokespersons muted the possibility that it could even be systemic.

The cases that came to light in the mid-1970s also made explicit the importance of economic, political and social contexts in the construction of social problems. At the time, concerns over juvenile crime and delinquency were increasing and there had been extensive publicity given to child welfare policy and social work professionals as a result of the failure to prevent the death of Maria Colwell in 1974. Changes in the organisation of the social services during the early 1970s also gave rise to questions regarding the effectiveness of child welfare structures. In addition, a political climate that had seen the decline of consensus also saw the increasing influence of a New Right ideology willing and able to criticise state social provision and liberal ethics. For some believers of New Right ideology, the issue of child prostitution was to become briefly a metaphor for the decline of morality under the combined influences of liberal immorality and a socialist mixed economy.

Media coverage of children becoming involved in prostitution while in local authority care and another case which received considerable publicity concerning a child prostitution ring operating from an amusement arcade (Playland) in London, tended to present this phenomenon in two particular ways. The first was that young girls were seduced, manipulated or coerced into prostitution by an older man who then lived off her earnings. The second was that girls entered prostitution through peer pressure and the desire for money to pay for a way of life that she would not otherwise be able to afford. The former left little space for an understanding of why girls might be unwilling to prosecute those who prostituted them and the latter continued to associate participation in this form of sexual abuse with blame of the child. Thus the victim/threat construction of child prostitution, albeit often in a more complex and socially aware manner, continued.

Importantly, the cases involving children in care during the 1970s made explicit the link between young people who abscond from residential homes or family homes, homelessness and commercial sex. Unfortunately, more recent changes to welfare benefits for the young, in the context of increases in single parenthood, divorce and reconstituted families, have exacerbated the precarious social and economic position of those children who experience severe problems within their families or who run away from home or care. One consequence of this has been an increased resort to informal economic activity, such as begging, drug dealing and prostitution (Dean, 1999; Melrose et al., 1999). During the 1980s and 1990s, research into child prostitution, in its attention to life chances and the realities of the choices available to some young people, has begun critically to problematise the historical links made between passivity and innocence, participation and guilt.

Research conducted in the late 1990s (Melrose et al., 1999) suggests that increasingly young people may be getting involved in prostitution through peer group networks. This work suggests that the character of child prostitution may have been changing at the end of the twentieth century and that the role of the pimp was perhaps becoming less important. Researchers were told more than once by agency workers and older women working in prostitution that 'the drug is the pimp these days' (Melrose et al., 1999). Regional factors may also be influential with regards to the methods by which young people become involved in commercial sex.

Conclusion

Long-term historical analysis has suggested that the circumstances that have led young people into prostitution over the last century amount, at worst, to physical or psychological abuse and/or neglect, and at best to the result of limited choice. Nevertheless, children involved in prostitution have often been portrayed as choosing to be involved in prostitution and therefore as bearing at least part of the responsibility and guilt for their involvement in such activity. Unable to fit the idealised mould of the white slave trade image, children involved in commercial sexual exploitation have too often been condemned as having 'unnatural' knowledge and experience and as being something other than a child.

Historically, it is clear that young people abused through prostitution have borne little relation to the fragile and coerced young things portrayed by writers like W.T.Stead in the late nineteenth century. Gorham (1978) has observed that the 'real young girls' who emerged from the rhetoric were 'unmanageable and flightly' in the 'eyes of their would-be reformers'. In 'the privacy of their minute books and printed annual reports, organisations which manage rescue or 'preventive' homes reveal that one of their biggest problems was controlling the unruly behaviour of the girls with whom they came into contact'. The historian of The Children's Society, John Stroud, has observed that the staff running the homes had to cope, in some cases, with what he describes as, 'wild, foul-mouthed, undisciplined children, many of them steeped in the practices of crime and prostitution' (1974: 106).

There are clear similarities here with the problems faced by social workers and other practitioners in trying to intervene appropriately with young people involved in prostitution at the end of the twentieth century and into the twenty-first. Ayre and Barrett (2000: 55) note that children involved in prostitution at the end of the twentieth century may not be adequately provided for by welfare agencies precisely because of the challenge they pose to the victim concept. As they state 'aggressive, streetwise, anarchic young people who steal and do drugs as well as prostitution do not conform obviously to our idealised image of a child in need'. As we enter the twenty-first century, however, and primarily as a result of pressure exerted by agencies in the voluntary sector, this situation is gradually improving. The government has recently issued specific guidance in relation to the treatment and management of child and juvenile prostitution (DoH/HO/DFEE, 2000).

The extent to which greater public discussion of children in trouble, and specifically children who are sexually abused through prostitution, will impact upon providing more appropriate responses to these children can only be appraised in time. It is clear, however, that much of the effective work in this area has been conducted by children's charities rather than by social services. Unfortunately, cultural attitudes change exceedingly slowly and the media continue to make unhelpful use of terms such as 'white slave trade' (*The Guardian,* 26 January 2002).

CHAPTER 3

Young People Exploited through Prostitution: A Literature Review

Susan Drinkwater and Helen Greenwood with Margaret Melrose

Introduction

This chapter attempts to draw together some of what we know to date about the commercial sexual exploitation of young people in Britain. As a result of a gradual, and often painstaking, acceptance of the existence of this problem, we are now beginning to establish a body of work around the subject (for an overview, see Melrose et al., 2002, all the bibliographic references in this volume and this chapter in particular). Although in the past it has been suggested that there was a paucity of services available for these young people (Barrett, 1995), the models presented in this book go some way towards demonstrating that this deficit is beginning to be addressed.

This chapter supplies readers with a brief literature review. The topics discussed are associated with both young men and women and relate to such things as:

- The legal situation.
- The scale of the problem.
- The aetiology of the problem.
- Differences and similarities in the situations of young men and women who become involved.
- Responses to the problem.

Limitations of space have meant that we have not been able to address the international situation. Suffice it to say, that the intensifying internationalisation and globalisation of the world's social and economic networks mean that the national situation is increasingly difficult to make sense of outside of the international context (see Melrose, 2000b). Indications are that an expansion of national and international trafficking networks promises to augment and exacerbate the problem in Britain (see Sangera, 1998; Kelly and Regan, 2000; Melrose and Brown, 2002; Melrose et al., 2002).

The legal situation: shifting paradigms?

New government guidance in relation to young people involved in prostitution was introduced in 2000 (DoH/HO/DfEE, 2000). Its effect has been to shift the focus of official concern from prosecution to protection. The guidance recommends that where young people are involved, or at risk of involvement in commercial sexual exploitation, they should be offered a welfare based response rather than a criminal justice based intervention. This has prompted a major paradigm shift in practice (Ayre and Barrett, 2000). Young people, initially at least, are to be brought within the child protection system – however, no extra resources have been forthcoming to effect this shift on the ground (Phoenix, 2002).

Additionally, the law has not changed and the activities of girls and young women involved in prostitution remain circumscribed by the Street Offences Act 1959. It is still therefore possible for a young woman, who is not legally old enough to consent to sex, to be charged with offences of loitering and soliciting (Palmer, 2001; Dodsworth, 2000; Melrose et al., 1999; Lee and O'Brien, 1995). This same absurdity applies to young men and boys although a different legal framework regulates their activities in prostitution. Under the Sexual Offences Act 1956, it is an offence for a man 'to solicit or importune in a public place for immoral purposes'. Just as the law does not distinguish between women and girls involved in prostitution, it does not distinguish between men and boys. Therefore, although boys under the age of 16 cannot legally consent to sex with another man, they can be charged with soliciting or importuning when below this age (Aitchison and O'Brien, 1997).

The position is further confused by a suggestion in the guidance that when attempts at diversion fail, 'it may be appropriate for those who voluntarily continue in prostitution to enter the criminal justice system in the way that other young offenders do' (DoH/HO/DfEE, 2000). The guidance recommends that a young woman should only be charged with offences of loitering and soliciting after all attempts at diversion have failed and she is deemed by the authorities concerned to be 'voluntarily' and 'persistently' returning to prostitution. The guidance also suggests that in these situations, steps should be taken to establish that the young person is not being 'coerced' (presumably by another person) into prostitution (Melrose and Ayre, 2002). Various authors have pointed out that, paradoxically, those young people who are most 'in need' are precisely those who are most likely to continue to place themselves in abusive situations. It is these young people who are most in need of care of protection, and punishment should not therefore be regarded as an appropriate alternative (Melrose and Barrett, 1999; Melrose and Brodie, 1999; Melrose and Ayre, 2002).

Scale of the problem

There is a consensus in the literature that information about the numbers of young people involved in commercial sexual exploitation is not available nationally (Barnardo's, 1998; Shaw and Butler, 1998; McNeish, 1998; Barrett, 1998; Ayre and Barrett, 2000). As a result of the clandestine nature of these activities we can only proffer conservative estimates, which suggest that the problem is more widespread than previously imagined (Brain et al., 1998) and may be escalating (Green, 1992; Kershaw, 1999; Melrose et al., 1999). The evidence we do have is fragmentary (Melrose and Ayre, 2002) since it is often based on small-scale local agency studies (Shaw and Butler, 1998). We do know, however, that this is not a problem confined to urban or metropolitan areas (Brain et al., 1998; Melrose et al., 1999; Melrose et al., 2002).

Home Office figures show that in England and Wales, between 1989 and 1997, 514 girls aged between 10 and 15 were cautioned or convicted for loitering and soliciting compared to 4,356 16 and 17-year-old girls in the same period (Official Criminal Statistics 2001 cited in Phoenix, 2002). This number represents approximately 10 per cent of all females arrested for soliciting during the period (Duffin and Beech, 2000). These figures suggest that the 'problem' of child prostitution is 'actually a problem of 16 and 17 year-olds' (Phoenix, 2002: 368). It has been suggested by a number of studies, however, that a large percentage of adult prostitutes become involved as juveniles (cf. Taylor-Browne cited in May et al., 2000; Skidmore, 2000; Melrose et al., 1999; Pearce and Roach, 1997).

Based on police and Home Office statistics it has been estimated that there are 2,000 young people involved in prostitution in any one year in the UK with one third being under 16. In London alone, 200–300 young people are thought to be involved (Bluett et al., 2000). It has been pointed out previously that official statistics notoriously underestimate the scale of any deviant activity (Lee, 1993), and those related to prostitution offences provide figures *only* for those who have been cautioned for, or convicted of, a prostitution-related offence. They do not take into account those who have not come to police attention. For this reason, other commentators suggest that up to 5,000 young people may be involved at any one time (Thompson, 1995; Crosby and Barrett, 1999; Ayre and Barrett, 2000). The estimated ratio of females to males aged under 18 who are involved is four to one (Thompson, 1995; Barrett, 1998; Ayre and Barrett, 2000).

We can accept that for several reasons it would be extremely difficult to calculate accurately exactly how many young people are being exploited in this way. The nature of these activities, combined with the methodological and ethical difficulties involved in carrying out research in this field (Melrose and Ayre, 2002; Melrose, 2002), impose their own prohibitions. These difficulties are further compounded by the fact that *very* young people's involvement often occurs out of sight – in massage parlours, private homes or saunas (Swann, 1998 and see Chapter 10 this volume).

Until the government introduced guidance in relation to the treatment of, and response to, young people involved in commercial sexual exploitation (DoH/HO/DfEE, 2000), the young people themselves tended to be defined as 'the problem' (Lee and O'Brien, 1995). As with other prostitution-related laws, the focus was on the children/women providing services rather than on the consumers of those services (Adams, et al., 1997; Faugier and Sergeant, 1997). Academic texts were therefore based on the premise that the young people concerned were 'deviant' (Coombs, 1974; James, 1976; Davis, 1981) and research in the UK, Europe and the US was conducted accordingly (Ennew et al., 1996). The young people therefore carried an historical legacy – or 'baggage' (see Chapter 2 this volume).

As a result of the new guidance, things have been changing recently. Those charged with responsibilities for protecting children have, at the same time, been charged with the responsibility of targeting police activities on the men who exploit them in prostitution (DoH/Ho/DfEE). And about time too, some of us might say.

The aetiology of the problem

O'Neill (2001: 84) has recently argued that: 'Routes into prostitution appear to be centrally related to economic need, association with the area, other working women, with men or friends and family that are involved'. In short, the evidence suggests that young people become involved in prostitution through a series of complex and interrelating variables that are almost impossible to disentangle (Cockrell and Hoffman, 1989; O'Neill et al., 1995; Green et al., 1997; Melrose et al., 1999; Ayre and Barrett, 2000; Phoenix, 2001). These variables include poverty and previous experiences of abuse and difficult or disrupted family lives and relationships. Experiences of residential care, drug use, and alienation from the education system and/or coercion by an abusive adult have also been found to be important (Melrose et al., 1999; Friedberg, 2000; O'Neill, 2001; Phoenix, 2001; Melrose et al., 2002; Phoenix, 2002). As Phoenix has recently pointed out, 'there exists a multiplicity of social factors that correlate with involvement in prostitution and funnel opportunities in such a way as to make that involvement plausible' (Phoenix, 2002: 362). These social factors are examined in more detail below.

Poverty
According to O'Neill (1997), the institution of prostitution cannot be understood outside of the social and economic context in which it is produced. O'Neill, along with Phoenix (2002: 361) and others (O'Connell-Davidson, 1998; Melrose et al., 1999; O'Neill, 2001) have argued that the bottom line in prostitution is 'always economic need'. With rising numbers of young people entering post-16 education and labour market demand for

employees who are highly skilled or trained, those young people who remain unqualified are 'left behind' (Jones, 2002) and become increasingly marginalised from the socio-economic, and political 'mainstream' (Green et al., 1999; Pitts, 2001; Jones, 2002).

Government legislation introduced in April 1988 saw benefits withdrawn from young people under the age of 18. Several authors have discussed the possibility that removing entitlements to benefits for 16–18-year-olds has inadvertently led increasing numbers of them to adopt informal economic activities to ensure their survival (Dean and Melrose, 1996; 1997; 1999; Craine, 1997; Dean, 1997; Melrose et al., 1999; Melrose, 2000b). For young women who find themselves without an income, it appears that prostitution often presents itself as an apparently viable alternative (Green, 1992; O'Connell-Davidson, 1998; Melrose et al., 1999; O'Neill, 2001; Phoenix, 2002). At the same time, these 'child hostile' social policies (Mayall, 1997) serve to block their exit routes once they have become involved (Green, 1992; Patel, 1994; Pitts, 1997; Green et al., 1997; Melrose et al., 1999). It has recently been argued that as much as prostitution may provide a route out of poverty for those who become involved in it, it serves at the same time to further entrench their impoverishment (Phoenix, 2001).

We know from previous work in this field that young people who become involved in prostitution are usually socially isolated and lacking the support networks that might ordinarily prevent their drift into self-destructive forms of behaviour (Pitts, 1997). Family breakdown and/or abuse and neglect have been cited as precursors to homelessness, often because these factors result in young people running away from abusive situations. Research has also demonstrated that young people tend to run away from the most destabilised neighbourhoods (Pitts, 1997). Going missing from home or care has been shown to result in poor education and problems at school. It can also lead to homelessness and social isolation and has been identified as a significant risk factor in young people becoming involved in prostitution (Stein et al., 1994; Lee and O'Brien, 1995; Pitts, 1997; Melrose et al., 1999).

Child sexual abuse

The link between young people's involvement in prostitution and experiences of child sexual abuse within and beyond the family has been well established by previous research (O'Neill et al., 1995; Lee and O'Brien, 1995; Melrose et al., 1999). Other work has also suggested that large numbers of adult sex workers have been sexually abused as children, both at home and in care (Faugier and Cranfield, 1994; Foster, 1991). There are disagreements, however, about whether the correlation can be seen as direct or indirect. Some commentators suggest a direct causation between sexual abuse and involvement in commercial sexual exploitation (McMullen, 1987; 1988). They argue that sexual abuse in childhood produces a loss of self-worth, which results in indifference to mistreatment by adults (Lee and O'Brien, 1995). Others see the causal connection less clearly (Seng, 1989; West and De Villiers, 1992; Widom and Ames, 1994; Nadon et al., 1998) and instead suggest that abuse triggers a chain of events, running away for example, which in turn can lead to prostitution.

Residential care

The connection between the residential care system, young care leavers and commercial sexual exploitation is mentioned repeatedly in the literature (Kinnel, 1991; Jesson, 1991;1993; Boyle, 1994; Benson and Matthews, 1995; O'Neill et al., 1995; Barnardo's, 1998; Farmer and Pollock, 1998; Melrose et al., 1999; Friedberg, 2000). Again, however, the relationship is complex and no direct causal link can be established (May et al., 1999; Melrose et al., 1999). Many young people who experience residential care have already experienced other debilitating factors – death of a parent, move to residential care, sexual or physical abuse, or exclusion from school and families (Berridge and Brodie, 1998; Sinclair and Gibbs, 1998).

There is also a suggestion that the social stigma and marginalisation that result from the experience of living in local authority care may make young people particularly vulnerable to commercial sexual exploitation (Kirby, 1995). In these circumstances young people may be exposed to others who are already involved and the concentration of young vulnerable people in these establishments has been discussed as a potential target for abusers (Lee and O'Brien, 1995; Barrett, 1997; Matthews, 2000; Palmer, 2001).

Drug use

The link between prostitution and drug use has been cited frequently in previous literature, but we are no nearer to understanding entirely the nature of the relationship (Frischer et al., 1993; De Graff et al., 1995; Miller, 1995; Kershaw, 1999; Melrose et al., 1999; Melrose, 2000a). Young people involved in prostitution will often use both drugs and alcohol, and it is widely acknowledged that the 'swapping' of sex for drugs is not a new phenomenon (Kohn, 2001; Green, 1992; Pettiway, 1997; Melrose et al., 1999; Dodsworth, 2000).

The debate lies in whether drug use precedes involvement in prostitution or whether involvement in prostitution precedes drug use. It has been argued, for example, that it is not uncommon for a young person to become involved in prostitution in order to support their own or another's drug habit (O'Neill et al., 1995; Melrose et al., 1999). This would seem to support a pre-prostitution drug use theory. At the same time, however, the evidence suggests that young people will often use drugs to mask the harsh realities of their lifestyle once they are involved in prostitution (Green, 1992; Kershaw, 1999; Melrose et al., 1999; Melrose, 2000a).

Evidently, more empirical work is needed in order to investigate both the direction and intensity of the relationship between young people's involvement in prostitution and their drug use. One common factor in the debate however, identifies drug abuse and dependency as major obstacles in trying to remove a young person from prostitution (Groocock, 1992; Melrose et al., 1999; Melrose et al., 2002).

Coercion

The part that coercion plays in ensnaring young people (usually young women) into prostitution has also been discussed in previous literature. For some commentators, this represents a major push factor in a young person's introduction to prostitution (Swann, 1998; May et al., 2000). This coercion will often come from an abusing adult, usually a 'pimp', whereby total dominance over a young person is achieved. This involves targeting vulnerable, socially isolated young girls in an attempt to befriend them. The pimp poses as the young girl's boyfriend usually demonstrating elaborate gestures of affection and generosity. Once her dependency on him has been established, the 'boyfriend' will begin to place demands on the young girl, which results in him introducing the idea of sex work to her. The groundwork is in place for him to establish absolute control over the young girl, eventually resorting to violence and possibly drug dependency in order to keep her involved in prostitution (Swann, 1998; May et al., 2000).

While some people argue that pimps play a major role in drawing young people into sex work, others argue that they are not the only influential figures in a young person's introduction to prostitution. Some commentators have argued that pimps are not as important as they were once thought to be in forcing women into prostitution (Faugier and Sergeant, 1997). Others have suggested that 'the drug is the pimp these days' (Melrose et al., 1999; Faugier and Sergeant, 1997) and that, contrary to popular belief, the majority of young people are introduced into prostitution through their peers (Melrose et al., 1999). More recently, research has also reported that the children of women working in prostitution are thought to be at risk of becoming involved in prostitution themselves. A number of adult sex workers have claimed they were directly introduced to prostitution through female relatives (May et al., 1999).

Education

The majority of young people 'working' on the streets, in addition to their difficult family lives, will usually have experienced major interruptions to their educational careers (Melrose et al., 1999). Those children who feel frustration at their circumstances will often express this anger through disruptive behaviour both in and out of school. This serves to isolate them further from any kind of support network, including teachers and peers (Brodie, 1998).

With no support, a number of children will turn to truancy, which ultimately results in their exclusion from school (Gibson, 1995). A number of studies have demonstrated the strong correlation between exclusion from school and diminishing life chances (Brodie, 1998).

Young people who are excluded, or who 'exclude themselves' from school and other key social institutions (Collison, 1996) also lack any kind of structured and consistent personal and sexual education. Young people need to be educated in a way that will allow them to *be protected from* sexual abuse and sexual exploitation should they ever be in a situation that requires it. This education should not only be directed at young people but also those in contact with them including teachers, parents and key professionals (Lee and O'Brien, 1995).

Sexual orientation
Interest has arisen in recent years concerning the numbers of young people involved in prostitution who struggle with their sexual orientation. Many (young) lesbians enter prostitution, despite the common myth that all prostitute women are heterosexual (Green, 1992). Many young men involved in prostitution define themselves as 'heterosexual' (see Chapter 8 this volume).

Coming to terms with their sexuality can be an ordeal for young people as a result of the stigma that attaches to homosexuality and lesbianism. According to Palmer (2001), denying young men the same rights as their heterosexual peers in relation to their sexuality, may inadvertently mean that they are given no option but to seek out alternative means of expressing or testing their sexuality. Altman (1999) who claims that 'young men may turn to prostitution as a way of expressing their homosexual desires which social pressures deny' supports this view. This may be an over-simplification, however, and would require further empirical evidence in order to verify it. One study, for example, suggested that there were 'no noticeable differences between males and females in terms of the factors which led them to prostitution and which they found made it difficult for them to get out' (Melrose et al., 1999: 13).

'Pull factors'
Just as there are various 'push' factors to take into account when considering how and why young people become involved in prostitution, so there are numerous 'pull' factors that may explain their continued involvement. Amongst these, drugs, 'power', money, 'excitement' have been conspicuously present in many accounts (Melrose et al., 1999). For many of these young people, vulnerability and abuse have been major features of their childhood. Through prostitution, they regain some 'control' in that they

may perceive that they have 'power' over the punters, and money to satisfy their own needs. They view their income as a measure of their own success, gaining a sense of self-worth because they are being paid for a service they are providing (Weisberg, 1985; Kershaw, 1999, Melrose et al., 1999). In addition, the friends and contacts they make while on the streets form an extended surrogate family, one they might feel they could not replicate should they exit prostitution and return to 'straight society' (Melrose et al., 1999).

The literature suggests that in many ways, the factors that serve initially to propel young people into prostitution are also the very things that serve to keep them locked into this way of life once they are involved (Green, 1992; Patel, 1994; Pitts, 1997; Green et al., 1997; Melrose et al., 1999).

Differences and similarities in male and female involvement

Throughout this discussion, we have attempted to look at youth prostitution as a whole, taking into consideration the factors affecting both young men and young women. Although research has focused predominately on girls and women (Green, 1992; O'Neill et al., 1995; O'Connell-Davidson, 1998; Melrose et al., 1999; Pearce et al., 2000a; 2000b; 2003; Phoenix, 2001; O'Neill, 2001) we are beginning to understand more about the involvement of young men and boys (Donovan, 1991; Gibson, 1995; Kershaw, 1999; Aggleton, 1999; Palmer, 2001; and Chapter 8 this volume). The literature suggests that there are certain differences between young men and women who become involved and it would be useful to highlight these here.

Firstly, it would appear that girls are far more likely to be targeted by an abusing adult or pimp than young men, as the process involves an abusive male exerting dominance over a young vulnerable female, in the traditional pimping model (Barnardo's, 1998). This model may, however, result from gender stereotyping in which young women are seen as dependent, vulnerable and helpless. This is not to say that there is an absence of a coercive figure involved where it concerns young men. Palmer (2001) for instance, suggests that young boys are often targeted by 'paedophiles' who will condition the child into prostitution activity from an early age.

Secondly, young women involved in street prostitution are likely to be more visible in their activities than young men who, due to the stigma attached to homosexuality, often work more covertly and share more of a group culture than girls (Palmer, 2001; Kershaw, 1999). This needs to be taken into account when considering the official statistics for cautions and convictions of young men (aged 10–17 years) for activities that constitute prostitution: the figures for 1995 show that there were just seven (Aitchison and O'Brien, 1997).

Thirdly, according to Palmer (2001) the age at which young men enter prostitution is, on average, earlier than that of young women and therefore the average age of boys involved is younger. Women, however, will work longer in prostitution, often into their thirties or forties and sometimes older, whereas the average age for men to exit prostitution is thought to be in their twenties. There is also a view that women are often more confident than young men in negotiating with 'punters' (Barnard et al., 1990; Palmer, 2001).

Regardless of these differences, the one thing that appears to remain constant in relation to young people's exploitation through prostitution is that the 'choice' to enter prostitution is rarely an informed one (Palmer, 2001).

Responding to young people involved in prostitution

The various elements that make young people vulnerable to becoming involved in commercial sexual exploitation suggest a need for services that are able to address a variety of multi-dimensional, often entrenched, and entangled needs. There is, therefore, a consensus within the field that multi-agency approaches are best suited to address the complex needs of these young people (Yates et al., 1991; O'Neill et al.,1995; Shaw et al., 1996; Barrett, 1997; Brain et al., 1998; Shaw and Butler, 1998; Christian and Gilvarry, 1999; Melrose et al., 1999; Schissel and Fedec, 1999; Swann, 1998; DoH/HO/DfEE, 2000; Melrose, 2001). A combination of voluntary and statutory sector provision is viewed as particularly appropriate.

It is also acknowledged, however, that the young people we are talking about are often distrustful of adults, particularly those acting in an official capacity, who may show an interest in their activities (Shaw and Butler, 1998; and see Chapters 4–10 this volume). Statutory agencies in particular are reported to be perceived negatively by young people (Christian and Gilvarry, 1999). This means that many of the young people involved may be unknown to agencies that could potentially provide support. This, combined with the mobility of the young people (Melrose et al., 1999) further complicates attempts to establish the numbers of young people involved, and makes the work of professionals more difficult.

It has been established by government guidance (DoH/HO/DfEE 2000) that criminalising young people is not an appropriate response to their involvement in commercial sexual exploitation as this can result in further isolation, diminish their self-image and make the possibility of exit less likely (Shaw et al., 1996). It has been suggested for instance that young people may fear that the police will return them to abusive environments (Adams et al., 1997) or situations that they detest to the extent that they would prefer homelessness and prostitution. In some cases pimps have been reported as being able to control young people by threatening to report them to the police (Lee and O'Brien, 1995). It has also been noted that social services responses to these young people have previously been less than adequate, in part due to a lack of understanding of the needs of the young people (Barrett, 1998).

It is possible to misunderstand their needs because, as Wellard (1999) points out, these are not on the whole, 'nice polite children'. It has been shown that this view of the young people concerned has historically inhibited appropriate service responses (Ayre and Barrett, 2000; Brown and Barrett, 2002). These young people have been characterised as, 'aggressive, streetwise, anarchic young people who steal and do drugs as well as prostitution' and as such they 'do not conform obviously to our idealised image of a child in need' (Ayre and Barrett, 2000). It is difficult, politically, therefore, to invoke public sympathy for these young people.

In response to these complexities it is necessary to consider the fact that most relevant legislation contains directions for various professionals to participate in decisions concerning appropriate services for them, for services to be needs led and for agencies to work together (DoH, 1991). Schorr (1989) suggests a need for flexibility and the ability of staff to form relationships based on mutual trust and respect, amidst a host of other desirable criteria, in order to respond effectively to this problem.

Conclusions

This chapter has demonstrated the complexities of the factors that lead to a young person's entry to, and sustained involvement in, prostitution. It has highlighted a number of 'push' factors that are implicated in a young person's involvement in prostitution. These include economic hardship, going missing from home or care, homelessness, drug abuse, experiences of previous abuse and/or coercion by an abusive adult. The chapter has also identified the 'pull' factors that serve to make prostitution appear an attractive option for particularly vulnerable young people. It is these 'pull' factors, the allure of a 'better life', that seems to attract some young people to this particular way of sustaining their survival. The accroutrements of a better life might involve; money, a home, a boyfriend with a 'nice car' – or even one's own (O'Connell-Davidson and Layder, 1994) – a sense of power (derived from having money or over the punters) – a sense of being loved or a sense of 'belonging' (Melrose et al., 1999). It is important to bear in mind that, in spite of their unconventional lives, these young people share the aspirations of the 'mainstream' (Dean and Melrose, 1996; 1997; 1999; Melrose et al., 1999).

We have seen that both young women and young men become involved in prostitution and that, despite subtle differences, the precipitating factors appear to be very similar. Protection of children must therefore be extended to all children, regardless of their sex, gender role preference or ethnic origin.

If they are to be protected, children need to be made aware of issues of personal safety, abusive relationships and sexual exploitation (Lee and O'Brien, 1995). There is a real need for an improvement in the provision of personal and social education in schools if the exploitation and abuse of more young people through prostitution is to be prevented. Furthermore, greater importance should be placed on the training of those key professionals involved in the care and welfare of young people, including teachers, social workers and the police. These professionals will then be able to act in a way that addresses the specific needs of those young people involved in prostitution (Palmer, 2001).

We have seen that there is a lack of adequate financial support and accommodation available to those young people who find themselves living on the street. It has been estimated that within six weeks of running away, a majority of young people will resort to petty crime, drug abuse or prostitution as a means of survival (Kirby, 1995). This disturbing statistic suggests a need for a 'safety net' to catch those young people who have run away from home, or who are otherwise vulnerable, before they resort to desperate measures. There is a need for more government funding to establish safe houses and accommodation for young people. This should include a counselling service run by professionals specifically trained to be responsive and sympathetic to the needs of these young children (Browne and Falshaw, 1998). Additionally, a greater awareness of the relationship between running away, becoming homeless and vulnerable to commercial sexual exploitation needs to be demonstrated within schools (Rees and Smeaton, 2001).

The government appears to have made some small steps in recognising the absurdities regarding the law in relation to child prostitution. It has, through its new guidance, highlighted the need for the child to be viewed as the victim and the adult, a sexual abuser (DoH/HO/DfEE, 2000). There is now a need to develop effective mechanisms and strategies to target the adults who abuse and exploit the young people concerned, and to demonstrate that such activity carries with it severe penalties. Otherwise, we are sending out a clear message that to abuse children in this manner is acceptable.

The literature suggests that in order to improve the situation for these young people there needs to be more than a multi-agency response whereby agencies including the police, social services, voluntary and statutory agencies work co-operatively. Parents and teachers need to work together to educate their children in order that they may be protected from sexual exploitation, commercial or otherwise. Politicians need to work closely with those agencies on the front line to see first hand the problems encountered by these young people.

In order to protect children adequately, there is a need to tackle both the 'micro' and 'macro' factors that underpin their involvement in commercial sexual exploitation (Melrose et al., 1999; Melrose and Brodie, 1999; Melrose and Ayre, 2002). To do this, we need to 'solicit the investment of all stakeholders – families and youth who are disadvantaged and in need of assistance, child protection officials and their agencies, other child serving organisations and their officials, and citizens and their communities – to work together' (Barter, 2001: 262). In this way, children and young people can be protected from predatory and abusive adults as well as from the 'social, economic and political forces' that affect them, their families and their communities (Barter, 2001: 263).

CHAPTER 4

A Multi-agency Approach to Exploited Young People: The Nottingham Experience

Sue Gregory and Ian Winton

Introduction

The commercial sexual exploitation of children through their involvement in prostitution, and the use of indecent images of children, is not a new phenomena but these issues have emerged more recently as public and political issues. For the purpose of this chapter, 'sexual exploitation' is defined as, 'children involved in prostitution, use or production of indecent images including photographs, films and internet'. The term 'children' is employed as defined in the Children Act (1989) to mean anyone under the age of 18.

It is now officially recognised that a multi-disciplinary approach is essential in dealing with these diverse and complex issues (DoH/HO/DfEE, 2000). In Nottingham, the early 1990s were characterised by growing concerns amongst front-line workers, including social workers and police officers, and in particular those street-based agencies working within the 'prostitute community', about the number of children involved in commercial sexual exploitation. It was estimated that over a 12-month period there were approximately 40 girls and 12 boys involved. Of these, 95 per cent of girls and 92 per cent of boys were white. Ages ranged from 11 to 19 with the majority being 15–17 years. The local authority looked after only two of the girls identified. In comparison, 75 per cent of the boys involved had a history of residential care. Nearly all the children (80 per cent) had a history of difficulties in school with periods of non-attendance or exclusion.

The 'bottom up' drive for change was recognised by chief officers in the police and social services and resulted in the establishment of the Police/ Social Services Department Agreement in August 1996. This agreement established the principle and practice that children involved in prostitution should be regarded as victims of abuse and should therefore be provided with care and protection. At the same time, it was agreed that the criminal justice system should be used to target the adult abusers. These policies were subsequently supported and ratified by the Home Office Juvenile Prostitution Policy and more recently, in *Safeguarding Children Involved in Prostitution* (DoH/HO/DfEE, 2000). The local agreements that had been developed were revised in September 1999 to ensure that the same attention was paid to those situations where children might be involved in the production or use of indecent images, whether in the form of photographs, films or through the internet. The remit of the agreement was also extended to include those young people up to the age of 21 years who are eligible for leaving care services.

Policy and procedural framework

The Police/Social Services Department Agreement forms the lynch pin of the relevant procedural and policy framework which is illustrated below.

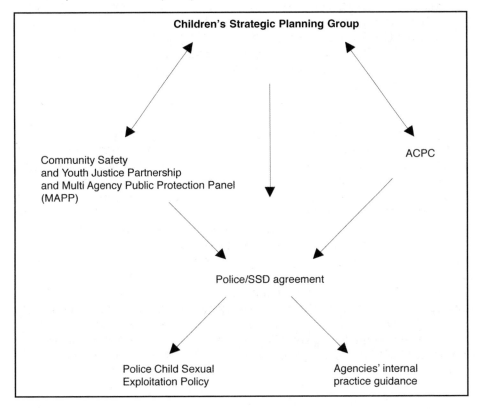

The underpinning principles of this framework are that:
- Children and young people are potential victims of exploitation and abuse and are therefore in need of services to support and protect them.
- Criminal justice agencies and processes should focus their attention on those adults who target, exploit and abuse children and young people.

These principles have of course been established through government guidance (DoH/HO/DfEE, 2000) in relation to the treatment of, and response to, young people involved in commercial sexual exploitation and the adults who abuse them.

The aims of the policies are straightforward and have remained the same since 1996. They are:

- To seek proactively to identify children who are vulnerable to sexual exploitation, for example, children missing from home or care; adults who befriend children while they are in residential care or who offer such young people 'open houses' in communities; children who are discovered in known 'vice' areas. All children found in these situations would warrant an 'Initial Assessment of Need' in accordance with the *Framework for Assessing Children in Need and their Families* (DoH/HO/DfEE, 2000). This includes gathering information from all agencies, talking to the child, family, as well as significant others, to agree a plan to protect the child.
- To respond decisively to support and protect the young people concerned.
- To disrupt and, wherever possible, prosecute the offenders.

While this framework has been in place since 1996, the emphasis of the work has clearly shifted from one of responding to children involved in prostitution, towards one of establishing systems to identify those children who are at risk of being sexually exploited as well as those adults who present the danger. It is of note that approximately 100 adults have been successfully prosecuted since the policy was implemented. The charges they have faced have ranged from kerb crawling and/or possession of indecent images, to abduction, rape and buggery. Sentencing upon conviction has varied from fines on the one hand, to one offender who received six life sentences, on the other. It is important to point out that *all prosecutions have been achieved without recourse to children giving evidence in court.* This has been made possible by the creative use of *all* currently available legislation and not just that specifically related to sex offences or children. Examples of this include Road Traffic Offences, Drugs Misuse Act 1971, Child Abduction Act 1984 and others.

The Nottingham approach

Sexual exploitation, including involvement in prostitution, is an aspect of a child's life that may bring them to the attention of statutory agencies and indicate a need for intervention. Many of these children are part of a wider group of young people who may be described as 'socially excluded' or 'disengaged'. As a result of this exclusion, they become vulnerable to commercial sexual exploitation along with offending, drug and solvent abuse and so on. Our experience locally would indicate that the early identification of sexual exploitation is essential, not only because we believe that all children have a right to be protected from abuse, but also because it is so difficult to intervene once young people have become entrapped in abusive situations. Furthermore, there is sufficient evidence of the complex problems these young people face, to suggest a need for a proactive, strategic response to this issue, which emphasises the need for inter-agency networking and a multi-disciplinary approach.

Although the establishment of policies and protocols provides a helpful framework for action, they do not in or of themselves effect change in practice or attitude. Such a vital and necessary change can only occur if it is facilitated and actively encouraged within each organisation that has a duty to care for these young people. Locally, such a change in practice and attitude has been achieved by proactively engaging *all* agencies within the authority. At the same time, we have built on existing work within the non-statutory sector. In particular we have developed our work with street-based agencies such as Prostitute Outreach Workers (POW), Base 51 (a drop in and outreach service for young people) and the GAI project (advice and information for gay, lesbian and bisexual young people). Local practice has been overseen by a multi-agency steering group, which was established in January 1997, and consists of representatives from all statutory and non-statutory agencies. This was achieved without complication by involving everyone from the outset, agreeing shared principles and establishing common agendas. Those agencies involved include housing, health, education, Youth Offending Team, voluntary sector organisations, probation, leisure and community services. Their input into the joint police and social services strategy is represented diagrammatically below:

All members contribute to the group and, at the same time, take responsibility for disseminating information in relation to this issue within their own organisations. This model of inter-agency working has created a network of 'lead' individuals or groups who act as 'advocates' for the issue as well as for individual children and young people. These advocates ensure that commercial sexual exploitation of children and young people is on the agenda for all agencies, and the local community, including elected members. This approach to the work has also helped to form a 'network' which has assisted in the identification of children at risk and the identification, and risk management, of those adults who target, exploit and abuse them. We are fortunate in Nottingham that we have a proactive anti-vice team which takes the lead role for the police, and who work closely with the Dangerous Persons Unit and the Child Abuse Investigations Unit.

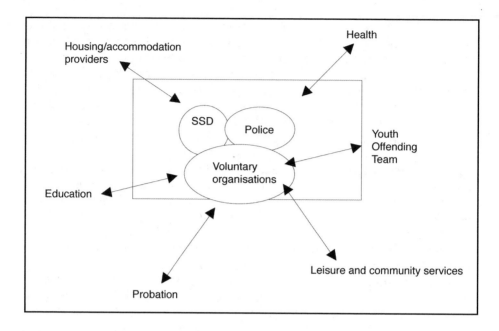

Identification and intervention

As part of our strategy, we have aimed to provide a continuum of services, which are integrated with mainstream provision, as opposed to establishing a specialist project. This has ensured that all statutory agencies accept responsibility and provide the services and support to which these children are entitled. This has fostered a culture of inclusion rather than exclusion. This model of working is illustrated below.

Prevention→Identification→Assessment→Advice→Services→Protection

We started in 1996 by completing an audit of existing provision, which enabled us, at the same time, to identify gaps in services to meet the needs of these young people. The following provides examples of work at each stage identified in the model above but is in no way exhaustive in recognition of continuing developments.

Prevention and identification

Prevention and identification work consists of a number of different elements, which involve the following:

- There is ongoing work to raise awareness and recognition, across all agencies and in the community, of the vulnerability of children to commercial sexual exploitation. This takes various forms, for example, training for those working with children and campaigns including briefings, printed materials and media strategies. Recent work has included a focus on the dangers of the internet, which included a presentation to all head teachers in the authority. Posters and stickers warning children of the dangers of the internet have also been produced and there has been a media drive to publicise a number of successful prosecutions by local police.

- There are named police officers from the anti-vice team responsible for each children's residential unit, including those which are privately owned establishments in the city.
- Specific initiatives have been undertaken by the police within the 'vice area'. In city centre venues such as public toilets and known 'brothels' and massage parlours, police have undertaken operations to determine whether children are involved at these sites and to disrupt/discourage illegal activity.
- The identification of those who target vulnerable children and the risk management of known abusers/offenders through the multi-agency Public Protection Panel. The authors of this chapter are both members of this panel.
- Addressing community safety issues such as street lighting, telephones for toilet attendants, disruption of kerb crawlers, meeting with resident associations to engage local communities and so forth through the Crime and Disorder Partnership.
- The provision and co-ordination of street-based and outreach work by POW in the 'vice area' and Base 51 in the city centre.
- We employ all new opportunities that are available to raise awareness and seek early identification of the young people concerned. Links have been developed, for example, with the recently established Education/Police Truancy team, the Pub/Clubwatch Scheme, and through Connexions.

Assessment
Assessment has two main aims:
- To ensure that all children have their needs assessed using the *Framework for the Assessment of Children in Need and their Families* (DoH, 2000). And in line with *Working Together to Safeguard Children.*
- The completion of risk assessments of those adults who exploit and abuse children. This involves using the existing expertise within Youth Offending Team, the probation service and the police.

Advice/services
The advice and services available to the young people include the following:
- Provision of mainstream statutory services including child and adolescent mental health services.

- Prostitute Outreach Workers (POW).
- A counsellor from NCH Action for Children operates a drop-in service and group work for young people on POW premises.
- A joint venture by Education and Base 51 has been established to provide for those girls who find it hard to access mainstream education.
- A drop-in for boys has been established co-operatively by the GAI project, POW and Base 51 in consultation with anti-vice officers and the social services department.
- A peer educator project, which is managed by POW and funded by the city council, Health Action Zone and private industry, has been established to work within one inner city estate neighbouring the vice area.
- Engagement of 'new' initiatives and opportunities when these arise, for example, Connexions advisors and Sure Start Plus.

Protection
Protection of the young people concerned, involves the following:
- The implementation of child protection procedures and multi-agency child protection plans.
- Assisting young people to move, in negotiation with their families, usually from the vicinity of the vice area and rarely out of the authority.
- In a very small number of cases, where it may be deemed necessary, the use of secure provision can be employed.
- The identification, targeting, disruption and, wherever possible, the prosecution of adults involved in the commercial sexual exploitation of children.
- The risk management of those adults identified as 'dangerous' through the multi-agency Public Protection Panel.

The majority of this work has been achieved by using existing resources efficiently and by making the best use of available skills and expertise. The multi-agency approach allows for available resources to be used efficiently and effectively, and also ensures that new opportunities are recognised when they arise. The approach facilitates a co-ordinated response whereby bids for new monies can be targeted rather than projects competing for the same pot of money. More importantly, from the children's point of view, it provides a choice of services. As a report on the Nottingham Child Prostitution Project has pointed out:

> *All those groups and organisations go someway to providing elements of necessary support to Young People to exit prostitution.*

> (Skidmore, 1999).

Experience and outcomes

Our research has identified a multitude of reasons to explain why children may be vulnerable to commercial sexual exploitation and become involved in prostitution. These range from basic survival and economic desperation to coercion and abduction by abusive adults. By making no assumptions about why the children we work with are involved, we provide an individual approach to assessing and meeting each child's needs. We have, however, found that the nature of male prostitution is often associated with networks of boys and adults and it is therefore important to make the necessary links and connections between the boys and the adults with whom they are involved. This is rather like putting a jigsaw together. To do this, we convene regular 'network meetings' which are assisted greatly by the police force intelligence bureau who 'map' the relevant links. These mapping exercises help to identify the most vulnerable children as well as the most 'risky' adults. They enable us to develop and agree strategies to intervene and to make provision for the delivery of appropriate services to meet the needs of the young people. It is also our experience that all boys identified are already known to the criminal justice system, and we therefore regarded it as a priority to establish a post within the Youth Offender Team to take a 'lead role' in this area of work.

While responding to each child and young person individually there are 'common themes' identified locally which are consistent with available research, including that conducted within the region (Skidmore, 1999). Many children identify money or drugs as reasons for involvement. We also have evidence of adults providing 'open houses' for vulnerable children seeking shelter and accommodation. This is particularly true of the boys we have worked with. Some children become involved because they are clearly seeking attention and affection. As one boy, Steven, a 16-year-old explained to his worker, '*He just hugs me and buys me clothes*'.

As expected, we know that some young people have experienced coercion and pressure including one adult male 'controlling' five boys and a 17-year-old girl who was systematically beaten to force her onto the streets. Children also talk of pressure from their 'peer' groups. Most of the 15 young people interviewed as part of the research conducted locally (Skidmore, 1999) said that they had been 'introduced to prostitution by others at the time they saw as a friend' (Skidmore, 1999). Children also talk about 'opportunity' in that many were exposed to prostitutes or 'dangerous' adults when they were vulnerable and/or needing to support themselves, for example when they were missing from home or care or when they needed accommodation.

Adult offenders

Adults have been prosecuted in relation to offences against children with charges ranging from possession and production of obscene materials, living off immoral earnings to indecent assault, rape, abduction and false imprisonment. Criminal investigations by local police have also initiated action against a significant number of adults by police forces across the country. An example of this was an investigation undertaken by the police, which started with a young person giving informal information about an adult providing an 'open house'. This led to the discovery of boys being 'trafficked' to London to make pornographic videos, which were then sold via the internet. As a result of this investigation, Nottinghamshire police successfully prosecuted nine adults and information about 25 different adults was sent to other forces across England, Wales and Scotland. Of these, one man was found to be in possession of thousands of images of children and young people and he was also charged with the abduction of a 14-year-old boy who was found in his house. Another man, who was found with thousands of indecent images of boys, taught at a private school – the list could go on. Successful conviction, however, cannot be regarded as an end in itself. Many of these adults have been, or are due to be, released from prison in the near future. It is therefore essential that we assess the ongoing risks they pose and manage them through the multi-agency Public Protection Panel. As with other sex offenders, these adults would be considered for treatment programmes while in custody. There are also examples where we have monitored contact and potential networking while in custody and we have therefore been able to put management plans into place on their release from prison through the Public Protection Panel.

Conclusion

Nottingham has developed a wide definition of sexual exploitation that recognises the links between prostitution, 'paedophiles' and pornography. There are some key issues that contribute to the ongoing success of this work and include the following:

- Good communication and information sharing amongst a variety of agencies.
- Early identification and intervention when a child is considered to be 'at risk'.
- The need for an holistic view of the child.
- A truly multi-disciplinary approach which recognises the skills and experience of all agencies and different professional groups.
- A flexible and responsive approach in the delivery of services to meet a child's individual needs.

- The early identification and disruption of those adults who target, exploit and abuse children.

We believe that the approach we have developed in Nottingham has been successful. Our evidence for this assertion is that the number of 'new' young people identified as being involved in prostitution has fallen significantly over the last four years. Additionally, only one young person (17-year-old girl) has entered the criminal justice system as a result of activities related to prostitution. There is further evidence that 85–90 per cent of young people previously identified have successfully exited from prostitution. Research recently conducted in the area (Skidmore, 1999: 16) concluded that 'the majority of those interviewed believed that they had been offered all the help necessary to help them exit'. One young woman had the following to say about the service she had received and the support she had been provided with by workers:

If I didn't know them (the workers) *I don't think I would be here now.*

(Sarah, 16 years).

In spite of our numerous achievements, we are far from complacent. Children will remain vulnerable and adults will continue to exploit and abuse them. We will continue to consolidate the multi-agency working to focus on prevention and early identification while ensuring services are in place to assist those who are abused through prostitution. In doing so, we will continue to seek new opportunities to assist in this work for example through Connexions, Sure Start Plus, Truancy Team, Pub/Clubwatch, use of CCTV cameras, and enhancing systems for responding to children missing from home. At the same time, we continue to tackle the abusers through proactive identification, targeting and disruption. Many of the systems in place to identify vulnerable children also assist in identifying the adults involved in abusing them.

All members of the multi-agency steering group remain committed to advocating for these issues. This includes ongoing awareness raising and educational work for all those working with children including members of the judiciary and practitioners in the legal system and those adults who abuse them. This approach is firmly embedded into the mainstream services of agencies within Nottingham and not dependent on a 'time' or 'remit' limited project. We believe this provides a solid base from which to meet the next challenge – whether it is an individual child, a dangerous adult or any other means by which children are commercially sexually exploited.

CHAPTER 5

The Sheffield ACPC Sexual Exploitation Project

Ann Lucas, Fiona Lothian, Marilyn Victor-Jefferson, Anne Byerley and Nicola Didlock

Introduction

This chapter seeks to describe a particular experience of attempting to deal with the sexual exploitation of young people, particularly young women, which was developed by Sheffield Area Child Protection Committee. We hope that by sharing information regarding our experience of the nature and extent of the problem of sexual exploitation in Sheffield, multi-agency groups in other cities may find something useful to inform their own work in this difficult and complex area.

We intend to give a brief description of the Home Office funded Sheffield ACPC Sexual Exploitation Project, and a brief history of what we knew about this problem prior to the Home Office funding. We then provide details of the procedures and protocols, multi-agency working, referral process, and police systems, which could be reproduced in other ACPCs. A profile of the young women referred to the project during the period February 2001–February 2002 is also discussed. Finally, we explain the nature of the direct work with referred young women undertaken by *Taking Stock* (the Youth Service part of the project), and SHED (Under 19s Substance Misuse Project), and detail our conclusions.

Sheffield ACPC Sexual Exploitation Project

The Home Office funded Sheffield's ACPC Sexual Exploitation Project, initially for a period of one year which was then extended to two years, from February 2001. The funding enabled the project to develop the work undertaken by Sheffield ACPC and to engage with young women at an earlier stage of their involvement in sexual exploitation. The overall aim of the project was to explore effective methods of engaging young women in order to encourage them to exit commercial sexual exploitation or to prevent them from becoming involved. The objectives of the project were:

- To enhance the ability of social services to chair and minute sexual exploitation strategy meetings and child in need planning meetings/child protection case conferences.

- To chair and minute monthly meetings of the multi-agency Sexual Exploitation Practitioner's Group.
- To create a police tracking system for young women subject to sexual exploitation strategy meetings in order to cross-reference their associations with each other and with adult offenders. This would enable the police to identify targets for prosecution.
- To collate data on referred young women in order to establish trends and patterns, for example, the significance of drug misuse, going missing from home or care.
- To raise awareness amongst all agencies by providing multi-agency training.
- To provide face to face work with young women through *Taking Stock* (a youth service based intervention).
- To provide drug advice sessions through SHED.
- To run a drop-in facility for young women who had already engaged in the direct work with *Taking Stock*.
- To produce an end of project report.

The history of Sheffield ACPC response to young people abused through prostitution

Because of the influence of a local campaigner whose daughter had been abused and murdered through prostitution (Ivison, 1997), Sheffield began work on these issues relatively early and our child protection procedure was launched in November 1998 – prior to the publication of new government guidance (DoH/HO/DfEE, 2000). When this was launched, we had no idea that the scale of the problem would be as great as it has proved to be. It is through concerted effort on the part of all agencies and having a clear policy and procedure to address the issue and raise awareness amongst professionals and parents that we have been able to discover something of the extent of the problem in Sheffield.

Early work
In August 1997, Association of Chief Police Officers (ACPO) pilot schemes were set up in Nottingham and Wolverhampton (see Chapters 4 and 6 this volume). We liaised with both schemes prior to agreeing our child protection procedure. This proved invaluable as a source of practical advice and as a means of learning about sexual exploitation generally. Between 1997 and November 1998 a child protection procedure was agreed between Sheffield Social Services and South Yorkshire Police which ensured that all young

people found soliciting on the streets would be treated as victims rather than offenders. This was also the beginning of the Multi-Agency Forum on Child Sexual Exploitation.

When negotiating and implementing a policy and procedure that challenges established views, it is important to remember that change is not immediate. In Sheffield, we had no organisational blockages to contend with, but the way we now operate has evolved as a response to our increased knowledge and experience. For example, our Sexual Exploitation Practitioner Group began in 1997 as a social services and police forum to agree the child protection procedure, which we implemented informally prior to the official launch. We quickly realised that to offer support to young people once they had been identified we needed a wider multi-agency group. Therefore, the Practitioner Group expanded in order to address the support needs of the young people we were trying to engage, for example, GU Medicine to address sexual health needs, SHED for issues of substance misuse and the youth service to provide individual and group work.

The procedure recognised that not all situations would be as clear as those in which the police found a young person soliciting. Other agencies were encouraged to contact the child protection unit if they had concerns that a young person was at risk. The indicators and patterns of behaviour alerting them to consider the possibility of sexual exploitation were clearly set out in the child protection procedures. Consequently, referrals were made to social services when young people were *at risk* of being sexually exploited through prostitution in addition to those made once they were actually involved.

Operation Insight

In March 2000, *Operation Insight* was launched jointly by social services; the police and NSPCC, in response to concerns that a number of girls aged 13–14 were at risk. The final report provided an analysis of information held on 80 young people who had come to attention through the child protection procedure. The report provided an analysis of associations between the young people and the adults identified, and associations between the young people themselves.

Operation Insight enabled us to develop a clearer picture of young women involved in prostitution. Of the 80 girls identified, 22 were involved in soliciting. Of these 22, ten were under 16-years-old when concerns were raised. Eight had been in residential care. All these young women were dependent on heroin or crack. A further 12 young women were involved in sauna work, work with escort agencies or by using mobile phones. The ages of the girls in this group ranged from 14–18 years with the majority being

16–17-years-old. 28 young people had connections to known pimps, drug dealers or adult prostitutes. All the men identified as pimps were also drug dealers. A number of young women were known to have been taken to work in other cities, suggesting links between pimps in Sheffield and elsewhere. In most cases, the young person had been reported missing from home or care on a number of occasions and for extended periods. Going missing from home or care was therefore considered a significant risk factor in becoming involved in commercial sexual exploitation.

Through *Operation Insight*, we developed a definition of sexual exploitation (links with older boyfriends for example) and an understanding of how it can lead to *commercial* sexual exploitation (prostitution). We came to regard links with older men and sexual activity with those men, as 'sexual exploitation'. Some of the men had links with known pimps. Sexual exploitation means that young women are at significant risk of becoming involved in *commercial* sexual exploitation. In Sheffield, we have thus far been unable to establish the extent of the problem of sexual exploitation of boys and young men.

The grooming process

This model of abuse through prostitution was developed by Barnardo's (1998) based upon their work with girls in Bradford. It demonstrates how a girl is targeted by an older man who becomes her 'boyfriend'. He gradually ensures that the girl becomes emotionally dependent upon him, initiates her into sex and detaches her from other influences in her life – friends and family – using emotional and physical violence. Eventually he sells her for sex usually from rooms rather than on the streets. This model is *one* route by which girls become involved in commercial sexual exploitation. There are other routes however, for example, needing money to fund a drug habit, being drawn into it by female friends, homelessness, and financial necessity. In Sheffield, nevertheless, we have found that involvement with an older boyfriend is a significant factor in young women's progression from sexual exploitation to commercial sexual exploitation.

Risks and indicators

These young people face immense risks to their physical, sexual, emotional and psychological health. The environments in which commercial sexual exploitation occurs have close links with criminal behaviour, drug and alcohol misuse and violence. In Sheffield, there have been three murders of young women exploited through prostitution in recent years. Young people also become vulnerable to other violent acts such as rape, physical and sexual assaults and coercion into pornography. Other risk factors can include physical injuries, depression, self-harm, and attempted or actual suicide.

An allegation that a young person is involved in commercial sexual exploitation should be considered carefully. None of the following indicators and patterns of behaviour should be viewed as conclusive *proof* of involvement but a combination of them may be suggestive of the possibility:

- Homelessness can lead to young people becoming involved in prostitution in order to survive.
- Financial necessity, especially when combined with homelessness, can be a precipitating factor.
- Drug and alcohol misuse may force young people to 'work' to fund a habit. Drugs and alcohol may have been used as dis-inhibitors in order to enable the young person to engage in selling sex.
- Experience of previous abuse not necessarily from within the family.
- Estrangement from family.
- Low self-esteem.
- Young people in care may be vulnerable for a number of reasons including: previous abuse; low self-esteem; searching for a loving relationship; being targeted by abusing adults; going missing.

A young woman's behaviour may change and these changes may indicate that she is involved in sexual exploitation:

- Forming links with older men.
- Forming a relationship with an older 'boyfriend' who may be a coercer.
- Secretiveness and hostility in relationships with parents and friends.
- Defensiveness – the girl may become hostile if any concerns about her activities are expressed.
- Going missing from home or care.
- Not attending school.
- An increase in health problems due to sexual activity or misuse of drugs or alcohol.
- Possession of money without plausible explanation, acquisition of clothing, mobile phone, other gifts without adequate explanation.
- Possession of excessive numbers of condoms.
- Reports that the young woman has been seen frequently in locations known to be used for the purposes of prostitution.
- Association with other young people or adults who are known to be involved in prostitution.
- Physical symptoms e.g. sexually transmitted infections or bruising suggestive of physical or sexual assault.

Sheffield ACPC child protection model

The Sheffield ACPC project is a multi-agency project that has built upon the relationship forged between social services, police and other agencies since

1997. The relationships with other agencies have evolved from recognition that only a multi-agency response can be effective in engaging with a group of young people that, for a whole host of reasons, are hard to reach. The project uses child protection procedures to identify young people at risk of sexual exploitation. Strategy meetings are held in accordance with Section 47 of the Children Act 1989 which causes enquiries to be made by the police and social services whenever a child is thought to be suffering significant harm. A child is referred to social services or the police whenever there are concerns regarding sexual exploitation, as the child will be suffering, or likely to suffer, significant harm.

Strategy meetings

Once a referral has been made to the project, a strategy meeting is convened and chaired by the Child Protection Co-ordinator. The strategy meetings seek to:

- Gather information regarding the sexual exploitation of the particular young woman.
- Identify support for the young woman and her family that will help her to exit from sexual exploitation.
- Agree a course of action in respect of any offender identified.
- Systematically gather information regarding links with offenders and young people. This wider strategy enables us to cross-reference associates and shows relationships between groups of people on a city wide basis. For example, we are able to find out which young women a particular pimp/boyfriend is, or has been, associated with.

Information sharing and attendance at strategy meetings

Under child protection procedures, information can be shared regarding the particular young person and adults who are allegedly involved in their sexual exploitation. Parents are usually invited to attend unless it is thought that they are actively involved in the sexual exploitation themselves. When parents are present, they usually give a great deal of information regarding adults involved with their children. Indeed, parents have increasingly brought the problem of sexual exploitation to the attention of professionals. Police information regarding a third party, however, cannot be given with parents present, therefore part of the strategy meeting is for professionals only. The young women can also be invited to attend the meeting although it can be a difficult process for them given the issues to be discussed. In addition to social services and police, workers from *Taking Stock* attend and representatives from other agencies as appropriate.

Police action following strategy meetings

Whenever a young person is the subject of a strategy meeting they are entered onto the police tracking system which alerts officers to the fact that they are vulnerable, and means that any information regarding that young person is collated. The young person is flagged up on the police system and links between offenders/pimps/boyfriends and other girls can be identified. If the young person is found with an offender, or potential offender, this will be entered as an intelligence record. Incidents of concern at the addresses where the young woman goes missing can be collated, and addresses can be recorded systematically for the police to check when a young person goes missing. The use of the Child Abduction Act 1984 Section 2 against the offender can be agreed at the strategy meeting. This is explained later in the discussion.

Social services action following strategy meetings

The social worker, in conjunction with workers from other agencies involved with the young woman, should complete an assessment using the 'Framework for Sexual Exploitation Assessment', which is an appendix to the child protection procedures. Following the strategy meeting, the case will be dealt with through convening a child protection case conference or a child in need planning meeting. Under Sheffield ACPC child protection procedures, a child protection case conference is convened only when the young person's parents/carers are actively encouraging the sexual exploitation or knowingly failing to prevent it. In the majority of cases the parents will be doing all they can to extricate their children from sexual exploitation and in these circumstances there is little to gain from convening a child protection case conference.

Sheffield's child protection procedures state that a child in need planning meeting should be convened to agree:

- A joint approach to the investigation of offences against the young person.
- The development of a 'child in need plan' which meets the young person's developmental needs and develops a strategy to support the young person in exiting from sexual exploitation. The child in need plan will be informed by the multi-agency assessment.
- Services necessary to support the young person and address any therapeutic needs they may have.

The young person may remain at risk of significant harm despite all agencies' best efforts because of continuing involvement in sexual exploitation. The child in need plan is reviewed regularly in this light.

Youth service action following strategy meetings

Taking Stock is the youth service response within the sexual exploitation project. It aims to create a safe space and provide an opportunity for young women who have been sexually exploited to 'take stock' of what is going on in their lives. An initial chat with them follows the strategy meeting. The young women, having heard about the project, are then able to decide whether they feel *Taking Stock* is something they wish to be involved in.

The majority of young women have chosen to meet with workers on a regular basis. Youth workers have found the reasons for this are:

- They have the choice to opt out at any time.
- Work takes place just with the young women and not with their families.
- Young women are offered a confidential service only reporting any new disclosures of high-risk behaviour.

Meetings with the young women take place in the most appropriate venue for them. They last an hour and are not based on a set number of sessions, as this is too rigid for the long-term issues they are facing. Time spent together is reviewed every six weeks so that the sessions are used most effectively. How time is spent depends on their immediate needs. Young women have been accompanied to the GU clinic, SHED, and BASE 10, an alternative to mainstream education that supports young people in short courses and facilitates their route to education, employment or training.

As well as providing information and advice, a large proportion of time is spent *listening* to the young women. This ranges from details of risky activity, feelings around professionals 'interfering in their lives', family life, issues with their friends, assurance that they are in control and crisis management on days when they are not!

The sessions work constantly to increase their self-esteem, self-worth and self-confidence by employing discussions, role plays, questionnaires and videos. The girls are encouraged to attend meetings held about them and to question decisions that are made about their lives. The work aims to provide alternative interests and give them choices. They are supported in making their own decisions about education, health, and future plans.

Measuring success is not straightforward. A young woman can go through frequent cycles of progress, maintenance and complete regression. The following indicators have been signs of positive achievements:

- Keeping in contact.
- Turning up for appointments.
- Making the journey to visit us.
- Popping into the project unannounced.
- Asking for help in a crisis.
- Disclosing more information.
- Attending review meetings.
- Going to an interview alone (e.g. college).
- Referring a friend.

Youth workers sometimes feel uncomfortable with their role because of the need to befriend a young woman, but at the same time try to find out more about the safety of the activities she is involved in. When a good relationship has been established a young woman often feels comfortable to disclose more details. Although it is made very clear that the work takes place within Sections 17 and 47 of the Children Act 1989, in language that they understand, it is never easy to make that disclosure having built a trusting relationship with the young woman. Fortunately, the relationships established have been able to withstand any initial feelings of anger or frustration that their information has to be passed on.

Because the relationships established with the young women are long term it is vital to set the boundaries around befriending from the beginning. If the relationship is to succeed, they need to know that although workers have supported them in very intimate details of their lives we cannot, over a period of time become their friends. The Child Protection system is a reminder of this. Workers remain in contact with young women whilst social services sees them as being at risk of sexual exploitation, and for as long as the young women are happy to be involved with *Taking Stock*, up to the age of 18.

SHED action following strategy meeting
Where issues relating to substance misuse are identified, a SHED referral form is passed to the named SHED worker. This mechanism ensures that appropriate interventions are offered. Throughout this process, the SHED worker liaises closely with other practitioners, ensuring a co-ordinated response where substance misuse issues are not overlooked.

Estimation of the scale of the problem in Sheffield and profile of young women

The referrals we have had for strategy meetings – the starting point for engagement with the project – range from girls involved in the 'grooming process' to young women involved in soliciting. We have analysed data on 63 young women, 13 of whom were identified during *Operation Insight*. Of the 63, we know that 14 are involved in soliciting. There has only been one young man referred to the project and therefore we are unable to draw any conclusions about the extent of the problem of sexual exploitation of boys and young men.

The tables on page 55 describe the ages of the 63 young women at referral (Table 1), their ethnicity (Table 2) and their living arrangements (Table 3).

Missing from home or care
Of the 63 young women, 43 have been reported missing from home or care. This bears out previous information from *Operation Insight*, which led us to

Table 1: Age

Age	Number
11	1
12	4
13	5
14	20
15	18
16	8
17	7

Table 2: Ethnicity

Ethnicity	Number
White British	59
African	1
Mixed	1
Not known	2

Table 3: Living arrangements

Living arrangements	Number
At home	40
Residential care	10
Living with relatives/friends	8
Hostel	4
Foster care	1

view going missing as a significant indicator of risk in becoming involved in prostitution.

The child protection register

Of the 63 young women, 20 have been placed on the child protection register. Only seven of the 63 young women were placed on the child protection register as a result of sexual exploitation. The remaining 13 had been registered previously, prior to the issue of sexual exploitation having been brought to our attention. The categories of registration are described in Table 4 on page 56.

When a young person is placed on the child protection register, a child protection plan ensures that the child is safeguarded and protected. As part of this plan, expectations are made of the parents, for example, ensuring that the young person is officially reported missing or co-operating with making a statement to the police in order to enforce the Child Abduction Act. The progress of the plan is monitored and reviewed. If the situation improves then the young person can be removed from the child protection register at a subsequent child protection review case conference. If the situation does not

Table 4: Categories of registration on child protection register

Category	Number
Sexual abuse	10
Neglect	7
Sexual abuse and neglect	1
Sexual and physical abuse	1
Physical abuse	1

improve, further action will be taken which may include a plan to remove the child from home by initiating care proceedings.

Substance misuse

Of the 63 cases analysed, 33 misuse substances, while 30 do not or we have no evidence that they do. Of the 14 young women known to be involved in soliciting, 13 misuse substances – of these, seven misuse crack or heroin. This suggests a significant relationship between soliciting and drug dependence, especially when this is heroin or crack. Our work with young people who are involved in sexual exploitation has highlighted that substance misuse is a factor in the following ways:

- As part of the 'grooming process' where young women are offered substances as a gift or bribe to draw them in.
- As a means of controlling the young women and instilling dependence on the substance and perpetrator.
- As a coping strategy to help the young women deal with past or current situations or events in their lives.
- Involvement in street soliciting to fund their own or someone else's substance misuse.

Interventions

All 63 young women have been the subject of strategy meetings, and child in need planning meetings or child protection case conferences to establish a planned intervention with the young woman and her family. All 63 young women, therefore, have an individual plan that attempts to meet their needs. The plan aims to encourage them to exit from sexual exploitation and includes a strategy for action to be taken against the offenders.

Engaging the young women to offer them support, to work with them to effect an understanding of the grooming process, and hopefully prevent them from becoming involved in commercial sexual exploitation is very difficult but it is possible with persistence. There is no easy or quick solution, however, as the girl will probably not view herself as at risk. Neither will she want to end the relationship with her older 'boyfriend', nor may she want to give up an established drug habit that she is working to fund. Work with this group of young women requires commitment, persistence, and the ability to remain motivated in the face of behaviour that continues to place the young woman t risk.

Interventions with offenders
The strategy to deal with offenders is crucial to the process of disengaging a young woman from sexual exploitation. During *Operation Insight*, evaluation of the data we gathered from engagement with young people demonstrated that they would not make a complaint to the police regarding offences perpetrated against them. The difficulty in getting a complaint was either:
- The young women's loyalty to their 'boyfriends'.
- Fear of the consequences of making a complaint, for example, more violence from pimps, boyfriends or their associates.

Due to the difficulties in getting a complaint against the offender from the young woman, we have employed the Child Abduction Act 1984 Section 2 as a deterrent to offenders. Here an offence is committed by taking or detaining a child under 16, so as to remove or keep the child from the lawful control of someone that has, or is entitled to have, the lawful control of the child. *This offence can be committed even when the child goes willingly with the abductor but does so as a result of an inducement. An inducement can be as simple as the offer of food or a bed for the night.*

The use of Section 2(1)(a) of The Child Abduction Act 1984 negates the need to rely on the formal complaint of a child. The parent or guardian provides a formal complaint, in statement form, to the police. By considering how the Act is used nationally, and through consultation with the Crown Prosecution Service locally, agreement has been reached on how the Act can be effectively implemented. The agreed protocol is as follows:
- Once a child is identified at a strategy meeting as being at risk, a decision is taken as to whether the use of The Child Abduction Act is appropriate. The young person is entered onto the police tracking system.
- A statement is obtained from the parent/guardian detailing who has parental responsibility, and the problems encountered by the parent so far, for example, the child going missing from home, the adult giving the child gifts, drugs, money and so forth. The parent states that they do not consent to the relationship or the individual encouraging the child to stay with them.
- The individual is served *in person* with a letter from South Yorkshire Police or social services stating the child's name and age, and that the

person who has parental responsibility does not give consent for the relationship to continue.

- The letter clearly places the onus on the adult to take steps, for example by contacting the police, parents or social services, to ensure that the child is not in their company *even if the child goes with them of their own volition*.
- The letter can be used in respect of children in care or accommodated by social services.
- By serving the letter the individual is aware of the nature of the offence they commit and that if their behaviour persists, arrest and prosecution are the likely outcomes.

Eight child abduction letters have been served on adults in the period February 2001–February 2002. There have been no prosecutions but the adults involved have not come to police attention with other young women and have often disassociated themselves from the original young woman. The use of this Act empowers parents who may feel unable to protect their child from an offender. Working in partnership and supporting parents is very important. Also, it is important to assess what is happening within the family in order to identify whether there are child protection issues to be addressed or whether the parents need Family Support Services to help them to set boundaries for the young person.

We continue to work on ways of prosecuting offenders, for the serious crimes they commit, without relying upon a complaint from the young person.

Training and awareness raising

The training and awareness raising sessions are one-day multi-agency events, which have attracted practitioners working at different levels in a variety of professional contexts in both voluntary and statutory sectors, for example, health, education, the police and social services.

The day covers:

- The history of the problem nationally and locally.
- Risks, indicators and patterns of behaviour and how these can be picked up by workers from all agencies.
- Details of Sheffield ACPC procedure in respect of young people at risk of sexual exploitation.
- How to make a referral for a strategy meeting to be held.
- Interventions effected through strategy meetings, child in need planning meetings and child protection case conferences.
- Loudmouth Theatre Group perform *Working for Marcus* and participants work with them on how to intervene to help a young woman exit from sexual exploitation.

- *Taking Stock* talk about their direct work with young women referred by strategy meetings.

Conclusions

From our work in Sheffield, we have learned a number of important things about sexual exploitation. We have achieved this by utilising existing child protection systems and ensuring that all agencies engaged in the protection of children and the promotion of their welfare are aware of the problem, and are willing to contribute to an individual plan for each child, which seeks to address their particular needs. We believe that although this is an extremely complex and difficult problem to address we have begun to make some progress. We believe that our model could be replicated in other ACPCs as the infrastructure is already there. We have outlined our main findings and the achievements we feel we have made below:

What has been learned regarding sexual exploitation in Sheffield?

- This is not a Sheffield problem but one that is hidden and needs concerted effort on the part of all agencies to uncover its extent.
- Young women face significant risks to their physical, emotional and sexual health.
- Young women are at risk through associations with offenders, drug dealers and pimps.
- There has been information from some young women that the people with whom they associate also deal in firearms.
- There are some girls as young as 12, who go missing from home on a regular basis, have contact with known offenders, and are being sexually exploited.
- The significance of going missing from home or care to risk of sexual exploitation has again been confirmed.
- Young women and their families are afraid to make complaints to the police because they fear repercussions from offenders.
- The use of The Child Abduction Act is a way of targeting offenders without a complaint from the young woman.
- There are close links between sex and drugs markets in Sheffield. The young women involved in soliciting all have a significant drug habit. The pimps also engage in drug dealing.
- It is difficult to engage these young women because they are very loyal to their older boyfriends or they are afraid.

Achievements

The following details the main achievements of the project:

- Raising awareness through multi-agency training events for practitioners and managers.
- The number of referrals has demonstrated the raised awareness.
- The chairing and minuting of strategy and planning meetings has enabled multi-agency responses to be developed that address the needs of the young women and target the adults involved.
- The Practitioner's Group has met monthly and has been well attended by representatives from statutory and voluntary agencies.
- A fast track to the GU Clinic for young women at risk of sexual exploitation has been established.
- SHED has prioritised work with young women at risk of sexual exploitation and referrals are made to a named worker who attends the Practitioner Group.
- The youth service has engaged in direct work with young women and formed links with residential units. In one unit, they have undertaken group work sessions.
- The Practitioner Group has established links with CPS and will work with them on ways of achieving the prosecution of offenders without using a complaint from the young women.
- Young women who have been the subject of strategy meetings are flagged up on police systems as being vulnerable. This ensures that if they are reported missing the police will actively search for them, and also that intelligence is gathered regarding their associates.
- The systematic collection of intelligence through the strategy meetings and the police tracking system has enhanced our ability to collate information about offenders. The information has been passed to a crime analyst to enable the police to identify targets for prosecution.
- A senior police officer has offered support in line with results presented thus far, and following the report from the crime analyst will offer resources in line with targeting identified offenders.
- The use of the Child Abduction Act has become an agreed South Yorkshire Police policy, which will ensure consistency when dealing with vulnerable young people.

There is no quick or easy solution to the problem of sexual exploitation. The 63 young women referred to the project between February 2001 and February 2002 have complex and multiple problems, which have made them vulnerable to sexual exploitation. These problems have been compounded by the fact that adult offenders have targeted them and preyed upon their needs for affection, attention, and excitement. The work with young women cannot be totally successful without a means of tackling offenders. As a society, we need to give a clear message to offenders that the sexual exploitation of young people is unacceptable and will not be tolerated. If this does not happen then simply offering support to the young person will not be effective.

The project must consolidate and build upon the work already undertaken. In order to do so, the following action points are necessary:

- The database and intelligence gathering needs to be maintained. It is hoped that police action will target offenders in line with the intelligence already gathered.
- Awareness raising amongst professionals through multi-agency training must continue.
- Establish an effective missing persons scheme to ensure early intervention.
- Begin preventative work with young people in schools in order to raise their awareness of the dangers of sexual exploitation and the grooming process.
- Develop work with young women from one-to-one work, to group work and the provision of a drop-in service. When we began the project the original plan was to offer group work. At that stage, however, the young women referred were not ready for group work. Some of the young women who have engaged with *Taking Stock* are now ready to progress to a group or drop-in.
- Continue to investigate the issue of sexual exploitation of young men, which at the moment is a hidden problem in Sheffield.

In conclusion, the risks faced by young people who are subject to sexual exploitation cannot be underestimated and cannot be ignored. The project has uncovered something of the problem in Sheffield which demonstrates that young people are at risk of significant harm from people generally outside the family, and we will continue to work in partnership to address this. These young people are children in need who are also at risk of significant harm. We have found a way of working which acknowledges the need for investigation under Section 47 of the Children Act 1989 in circumstances where the risk is not from the parents. We must continue to keep that risk in mind even though a child protection conference is not convened in these circumstances. Social services have traditionally become involved in situations where the problems and risks have come from the family. The situations of young people at risk of sexual exploitation do not often fit into this category. We need to continue to move forward with a multi-agency approach that we firmly believe can be effective in achieving better outcomes for young people.

Our model uses the infrastructure of the child protection system, and we believe it can be replicated in other areas through Area Child Protection Committees. We hope that our experience will prove useful to other professionals and will at least give some food for thought.

A multi-agency approach is vital to achieving effective processes and plans to support young people involved in sexual exploitation. It is therefore essential to have a structure in place that ensures that all agencies are working to a common aim. The formation of a multi-agency group, under the auspices of the ACPC is one method that we have found to be effective.

Appendix 1 Agencies involved with the Sheffield project

Supported by Sheffield First for Safety a bid for Home Office funding for the Sheffield ACPC Sexual Exploitation Project was made. This bid was successful.

The agencies forming the ACPC Sexual Exploitation Project under the Home Office funding are:
Sheffield City Council Social Services Department (Child Protection),
Sheffield Futures and Connexions Youth Service
South Yorkshire Police (Escafeld House Sexual Offences and Child Abuse Unit and West Bar Plain Clothes Department)
Turning Point/SHED Young People's Drug and Alcohol Project

However, through the membership of the multi-agency Sexual Exploitation Practitioner's Group which meets on a monthly basis, the following agencies are also involved in the work of the project, and provide services and support to young people as part of a plan to help them to exit:

- Social Services (Family Support Service and Residential Units)
- Sheffield City Council Education Department
- Sheffield Health (representation from GUM and the Youth Clinic)
- Sheffield Youth Offending Team
- Sheffield Futures and Connexions
- CROP (Coalition for the Removal of Pimping)
- SOVA CAST (Befriending Project)
- SWWOP (Sheffield Working Women's Opportunities Project)
- Crown Prosecution Service
- Sheffield City Council Housing Department

The Practitioner Group provides a forum for representatives to discuss issues arising from practice, and also a means to change practice in the light of our ongoing experience. Relationships between the agencies are excellent and we are all committed to finding solutions to what is an extremely difficult and complex issue to tackle.

The Practitioner Group reports to the ACPC Reference Group which meets three monthly and has representation from senior managers. Any difficulties encountered in practice can be taken to this group.

CHAPTER 6

Young People and Prostitution: The Response from Wolverhampton

Tom Duffin

Introduction

What must it be like? Just another problem for society to wrestle with or a thought provoking issue illustrated in an item on the evening news? The truth is, most of us cannot know what it is like to be a child and exploited in prostitution. Close your eyes and think of a time in your life when you have been really low – perhaps a time when you felt lonely and not cared for. The loss of a dear friend or relative perhaps. Increase the intensity of that emotion by a factor of ten. Out of the darkness, a glimpse of light appears at the end of the tunnel. A friendly face, someone who appreciates you – someone who can give you affection and time. Someone who talks with you and not at you. And that is where the end to the loneliness starts. It may end with death, a wrist partly severed with a carving knife, being dangled from the top of a block of flats, gang rape, or just a series of brutal beatings. It should be no surprise then to realise that the standard range of options for access and intervention for young people abused through prostitution consistently fail to meet the needs of one of the most vulnerable groups in our society.

Experience from a dedicated Barnardo's project 'Streets and Lanes' (Barnardo's, 1998) and the Children's Society's report 'The Games Up' (Lee and O'Brien, 1995) led the police service to reflect on its response to children who become involved in prostitution. An Association of Chief Police Officers (ACPO) spokesperson was appointed to address this issue. The spokesperson rapidly formed a group to review statutory responses to the difficulties children face when they become involved in prostitution. The group produced an agreement between ACPO and the Association of Directors of Social Services (ADSS) on joint responses to children involved in prostitution. The methodology was tested in two pilot sites, in Wolverhampton and in Nottinghamshire. This chapter will reflect on the experiences and learning from the work in Wolverhampton.

Historical perspective

At the start of the project in Wolverhampton, those involved asked themselves two questions: firstly, is it true that children who become involved in prostitution suffer in the acute manner described by the Barnardo's report? And secondly, if it is true, is there anything that can be done to tackle it effectively?

In a study of the city's prostitution problem, it was reported that Wolverhampton had the third highest concentration of street prostitutes in the country (Edwards, 1991). Historically, the origins of the prostitution problem are reported to date back to early Victorian times when large numbers of migrant labourers came to the town to work on the newly constructed railway. Statistical evidence reveals a consistently high number of vice related arrests in the town over the years (Edwards, 1991). During the 1970s and 1980s, Wolverhampton saw industrial decline and had unemployment figures above national and regional averages. In 1990, the town was reported to have one of the largest numbers of single parent households in the country (Edwards, 1991).

Traditional police response

In policing terms, the problems associated with prostitution had previously been addressed predominantly by enforcement. The problem was identified by complaints from residents in relation to nuisance and the visible presence of women on street corners, a few of whom were under 18. During the early 1990s, each year there were in the region of 2,000 arrests for loitering for prostitution, involving about 200 different women. About 10 per cent (20) of those women were under 18 years of age. At that time, enforcement was the main focus of police activity. Although it was not the only focus, persistent complaints about women loitering and used condoms being discarded in residential areas led to what appeared to be a rational response. Enforcement activity was also aimed at men who bought sex from prostitutes with about 70 prosecutions for soliciting women (or kerb crawling) per year. The details of these men and their convictions were reported in local newspapers. There were also about 12 prosecutions per year for living on the earnings of prostitution, exercising control and direction over prostitutes or assault (Whitehouse et al., 1991–98). None of the prosecutions related to offences against children. A review of these cases showed that in over two-thirds of them, complaints had been withdrawn, the most serious charges had been discontinued or aggravating features had not been presented in evidence.

The police effort to tackle the problem was delivered through a small, dedicated vice squad. This had been established for well over a decade and as the statistics reveal, was primarily focused on making large numbers of arrests.

Professionals across a range of caring agencies had concerns about a small number of children. Children, who it appeared, may have been lured and seduced into unpredictable and unstable lifestyles. There was a high level of teenage pregnancy and vice squad officers occasionally encountered young girls on the streets. The girls were offered intervention and genuine attempts were made to divert them from prostitution. Most were not seen on the streets again, having learned their lesson, or so it was assumed. A few, however, went on to become regular faces.

New ways of working

Since August 1997, children (under the age of 18) suspected of being involved in prostitution, who come to the notice of the police in Wolverhampton have been subject to different interventions. Home Office Circular 109/59, which governed the cautioning of prostitutes, was suspended in respect of children under 18 and the principles of 'working together' in cases of child protection were adopted. A local agreement was developed, based on the national ACPO/ADSS guidance. The local Area Child Protection Committee (ACPC) formed a small group to monitor progress on behalf of the partners who shared responsibilities for child protection, including social services, health, police and voluntary sector. Whenever information came to the attention of the police or social services that a child may be involved in prostitution, a multi-agency meeting was convened within two working days to discuss a strategy for protection, investigation and intervention. In practice most of this information was initially gained by police observation in vice areas but as the pilot developed, information was also generated from a range of other sources.

The police staff involved consisted of a sergeant and six constables who formed a local vice squad. The individuals brought different skills to the team: two staff had former vice work experience; two other staff had former experience as specialists in child protection. On occasions, staff with specialist skills were commissioned to undertake discrete pieces of work. On other occasions, skills were developed through on the job training or with the aid of bespoke training packages. The police staff worked closely with colleagues in social services (in particular the custodian of the child protection register), health (in the form of the senior nurse responsible for child protection) and a health worker dealing with adult working women through outreach services. The collaborative effort was facilitated through a protocol that enabled information exchange. This soon progressed into a number of close and constructive professional working relationships built upon mutual respect, trust and confidence shared between a few significant named individuals acting as a single point of contact and offering expertise at a senior operational level in each agency.

Results

At the start of the pilot work, we discussed the potential scale of the problem. During 1996, 23 children (under 18) came to the notice of the police in Wolverhampton. Two of those became regularly involved in prostitution and the others were seen once or twice. None reported being forced into prostitution. During the twelve months ending 31 July 1998, 66 children were identified as being at risk through prostitution. All of the children were female. Data on ethnicity was not captured. The ages of the children encountered are shown in Table 1 below:

Table 1: Ages of children identified

Age	Number of children
12 years	4
13 years	4
14 years	15
15 years	15
16 years	13
17 years	15

The results of interventions are summarised in Table 2 below:

Table 2: Summary of interventions

Number of cases	Result of intervention
17	Children made witness statements concerning being forced into prostitution. All of them were willing to attend court.
26	Children reported being forced into prostitution, but were not willing to make formal complaints or attend court.
15	Children are strongly suspected of being forced into prostitution, but did not disclose any information.
8	Cases involve referrals where there would appear to have been genuine concern for a child but enquiries suggest that the children had not been at risk through prostitution.
10	Children strongly suspected of still being involved in prostitution.
18	Fifteen men and three women were charged with serious criminal offences.

After a further six months there had been a total of 89 referrals and a total of 32 adults had been charged with serious offences against children. The offences charged included:

- rape
- kidnap
- unlawful imprisonment
- unlawful sexual intercourse
- attempting to procure a child for unlawful sexual intercourse
- conspiracy to pervert the course of justice
- procuring a child for the purpose of prostitution
- assault
- witness intimidation
- perverting the course of justice
- living on earnings of prostitution

Many of these cases resulted in the perpetrators receiving substantial terms of imprisonment. In one case, a man was sentenced to ten years imprisonment. In others, three and four year sentences were common. Only in isolated cases were other than custodial sentences received by those involved in abusing children through prostitution. The offenders were typically violent and had the potential to intimidate victims and professionals. With thorough investigation before arrest, it was often possible to secure remands in custody from the time of arrest until sentence. In order to achieve this officers would attend each and every hearing. They would brief crown prosecutors in detail about the levels of violence and coercion involved and support them by giving evidence, if necessary, to secure remands in custody. This reduced the risk of witness intimidation and also enabled victims and witnesses to recognise that they could be supported which enabled them to gain confidence in criminal justice processes. The most vulnerable witnesses were moved out of the area. They were escorted by police officers to and from court hearings and provided with accommodation out of the area during the trial. In the majority of cases, offenders admitted their guilt, often on the day of the trial. The victims made very credible witnesses but thankfully, they were generally not required to give evidence, because of the weight of the prosecution case.

The change in working arrangements in Wolverhampton led to the disclosure of previously unreported serious criminal offences. Serious criminal offences, like those mentioned above, were reported by children and young people who now had the confidence to tell someone what was happening. The victims could see that something was being done to help them and to stop the abuse. It was often a challenging situation to manage, as many victims still had a deep affection for those who were charged with abusing them.

In some cases, a substantial amount of additional effort was required to investigate cases under this scheme and this resulted in other areas of work being sacrificed for short periods of time. In a geographical area where it had been common for there to be significant enforcement activity, the complaints from members of the public rose. Experience showed that often individuals were comforted when they realised that police time was being spent investigating cases of children being abused and coerced into prostitution, rather than dealing with the visible representation of a young girl loitering.

The results of the pilot work suggested that in the past the police, and other agencies, had largely failed to respond, or responded inappropriately, to the difficulties these children faced. Often this was hampered by the fact that children and carers did not report their concerns. Locally there was a need for committed professionals to be creative and radical in delivery of services to ensure that obstacles could be overcome.

The problems commonly experienced by child victims encountered during the pilot included:

- Very strong emotional attachment to offending adult.
- Coercion.
- Economic survival.
- Stigmatisation.
- Drug addiction or other health problems.
- Frustration concerning previous experience of independence.
- Alienation from the family (especially fathers).
- Radical change in life structure – sleeping hours, social environment.
- Debt.

The difference effected by the intervention

As a result of the changes brought about by the work of the pilot, something startling had happened. Children who once suffered in silence now shared their problems with professionals. Concerned teachers, relatives and friends now had somewhere to go to discuss their suspicions or concerns. Victims and witnesses received protection and enhanced support. The intervention had made a significant difference.

On reflection, the provision of service to this client group was transformed. In reviewing what happened and how, a model of change (Kotter, 1995) was adapted and informed the following:

Urgency

A sense of urgency was established. One day, during a vice squad team briefing to discuss the new working arrangements, the telephone rang. It was the mother of a young girl calling because she was concerned about a man who was forcing her daughter to work in a sauna in London. All of the issues that were being discussed came home in an instant and the team leapt into action. Radical action was called for and officers arrested a man, following a car chase, who was about to transport a young woman to London. At this time, there was no complaint from the young woman. The girl was too frightened to say anything, but the officers suspected what was happening and knew enough to justify the arrest. Having removed the man, the girl decided to talk to the officers about what had happened. He was charged with offences including procuring a woman for the purpose of prostitution, living on the earnings of a prostitute and four cases of assault. Whilst he was in custody pending trial another young woman came forward to report what had happened to her. The man was charged with a further case of assault and attempting to procure a woman for the purpose of prostitution. The man was remanded to prison pending trial. He was subsequently found guilty and sentenced to three and a half years imprisonment. Further enquiries revealed that this man could be linked to 14 other children who had been involved in prostitution.

Within the context of this work, a degree of urgency was created among key individuals. That energy was harnessed and promoted throughout the project at all levels. Kotter (1995) quotes a former Chief Executive Officer who is reported to have said that the purpose of this was, 'to make the status quo seem more dangerous than launching into the unknown'. Clearly, if children were suffering serious abuse and agencies were responding inappropriately, then the status quo was far more dangerous than the unknown. The serious nature of the problems faced by the children in these circumstances was recognised for the first time. That degree of urgency was not manufactured in Wolverhampton but emerged in the early stages of the work. Two key members of staff from Wolverhampton visited a Barnardo's children's project in the North of England and spoke to staff about their experiences of working with children involved in prostitution. The staff described serious abuse suffered by children and revealed difficulties that they had experienced in accessing appropriate policing and other services. The Wolverhampton staff later reflected on the problems experienced in accessing the police and considered the causes and potential solutions. As children involved in prostitution began to disclose similar abuse in Wolverhampton, staff discussed tackling abusing adults and anticipated some problems. These were similar to the problems that had been reported by the staff from the Barnardo's project. There was a recognition that practice needed to change. In this case, the national pilot offered a unique opportunity to demonstrate that something could be done to help these children. Monitoring by the Home Office Police Research Group and a joint

Department of Health/Home Office review of child protection procedures, which was being conducted at the time of this work, also provided motivation to make rapid progress.

Coalition

A powerful coalition was created. In fact, there was already a powerful coalition in existence. There were three key roles in leading the change. At an executive level the Assistant Chief Constable (Operations) in the force was the ACPO spokesperson on prostitution. At a local level, the command unit operations manager (Chief Inspector) was tasked with delivering the project. An identified sergeant was team leader for a group of six staff who were responsible for vice-related policing issues across the boroughs of Wolverhampton.

The nature of the work was such that a collaborative approach was required. The local ACPC provided the opportunity to engage with key members of other agencies and gain their support. In each agency, a named person also had responsibility for this area of work.

Changes in key members of staff threatened progress. The Assistant Chief Constable moved forces on promotion, the sergeant team leader changed role after the first twelve months and other organisational changes impacted on staff postings. The creation of the powerful coalition was crucial, but maintaining it over a long period of time was not possible and there were delays and occasional difficulties as a result.

Vision

A vision was created. One of the difficulties in creating a clear vision in the early stages of a transformation is that the detail of the outcome is not always apparent. Issues that staff were concerned about were, 'Where will I work?' or 'How will it affect my job?' This work was a reflection of a transformation that occurred rather than the implementation of a prepared change and that was no doubt an inhibiting factor in promoting a clear vision. In practice, the vision emerged as something as broad as 'Protect children and tackle abusing adults and be radical'.

The vision was communicated to others. The vision was marketed with some success internally but with greater success externally. A positive media strategy meant that regular newspaper reports and television news reports and features helped promote the vision. The main police effort was delivered by a small number of dedicated staff and it is perceived that there is still a need to win the 'hearts and minds' of a certain proportion of the workforce. An example of successful marketing was a regional news broadcast that resulted in prime time television exposure and a large increase in the number of referrals.

Empowering people

Other workers were empowered to act on the vision. It became apparent that as traditional methods of response had failed, alternative options were required. Something had to be done to solve the problems that had previously been identified. Whilst imposing strict ethical guidelines on work, staff were encouraged to think and work differently. As a matter of policy, it had been practice generally not to effect an arrest for an offence until a formal complaint had been made. It was perceived that some children were too frightened to disclose what had happened to them. Therefore, on some occasions when abuse was suspected, staff made an immediate arrest and sought evidence of complaint *after* the perceived threats of intimidation had been reduced. In other cases, processes for fast-tracking out of borough placements for those most as risk were introduced.

The crimes disclosed frequently involved children being transported to different parts of the country. The staff involved in the pilot recognised the trauma that these young people had experienced. They developed the ability to engage children and give them enough confidence to report what had happened to them. Staff were enabled to respond more appropriately and in non-judgmental ways to clients who presented with some very challenging behaviour. The enquiries were often such that it was considered inappropriate for officers not familiar with the pilot scheme to conduct them. They often involved obtaining evidence, which was critical to the prosecution case, from persons who, if not involved in other criminality, inhabited a culture that was unlikely to be supportive of the police action in the first instance. Officers travelled to other parts of the country and gained valuable evidence.

In determining how best to effect change, one's judgement will be affected by one's assumptions about human behaviour. In practice, however, empowering staff provides the opportunity to involve the skills and expertise of all staff to solve complex problems and, in large and diverse organisations, this is essential.

Quick wins

Short-term wins were planned for and created. Activity was monitored monthly. The people suspected of being the most serious abusers were prioritised. A corroborated disclosure from a young victim was viewed internally as a success. When accompanied by a formal complaint, that was an even greater success and investigations into allegations against abusing adults were conducted meticulously. In appropriate cases officers sought to remand offenders in custody awaiting trial. Whenever an offender was charged or convicted there would be publicity generated. Early success was widely reported. This had the effect of increasing staff confidence in their ability to solve problems and it also encouraged more victims to report crimes. The individual arrests also served as milestones to staff in partner agencies who recognised that they could intervene to help children they suspected of being abused through prostitution.

Improvements in practice were consolidated and still more change was produced. One of the risks of reporting success in the form of short-term gains is that the perception can be created that the change has happened and that the problems have been solved. In the pilot work, these risks were minimised by the national review of the *Working Together to Safeguard Children* (DoH, 1999) guidelines, but other changes have meant that the status or perceived value of the transformation may vary over time. This needs to be managed if permanent change is desired.

New approaches formalised

The new approaches developed as a result of the pilot were institutionalised. The new way of working is agreed ACPO policy. The principles have been established in local working practices but *it is important that they become institutionalised so that they do not disappear when key staff change*. Nationally, the results of the pilot have informed a review of guidance issued by the Department of Health and the Home Office (DoH/HO/DfEE, 2000). This has meant that already a significant number of police forces have formed joint agreements with other agencies about protecting children at risk of abuse through prostitution.

Locally, the work of statutory partners evolved into a new project led by a voluntary organisation. After three years that project was terminated. Something was different and the anticipated outcomes were not achieved. This challenge still presents itself in Wolverhampton. In May 2002 a new police led initiative was formed. It has already won dedicated support from a voluntary organisation and other statutory partners are keen to improve practice in this area. In the first month, two adults have been charged with serious offences against children and both are remanded in custody.

From the experiences in Wolverhampton, the following key points have emerged:
- Children do not enter prostitution voluntarily. Professionals in the field will have different opinions about the reasons why children become involved in prostitution. There is often a range of influencing factors, but there is always an abusing adult nearby.
- There is a lot that agencies can do. Individuals and agencies sometimes feel powerless to act against ruthless criminals who exploit children but the pilot led to significant achievements.

- Inter-agency co-operation is essential. The challenges presented in each case are immense and it is only by close joint effort that real progress can be achieved.
- Identified key staff are needed to initiate action. Carefully selected and committed staff acting as a single point of contact in each agency is necessary in order to make progress.
- There are knowledge gaps in every profession. At times of difficulty it is all too easy to blame another professional, another agency or the system. In Wolverhampton, there was recognition that each agency had an opportunity to learn and improve service delivery. Attitudes need to change. The young people concerned often present as 'unruly criminals'. It is not until the true circumstances are revealed that they are recognised by most as tragic victims of acute abuse. Non-judgmental interventions can work.
- Develop trust and confidence with the young people. This can be very difficult when the victims are traumatised by violent coercion.
- Be persistent but don't rush them. In one case, two young girls were visited each day for six weeks until they felt comfortable enough to talk about what had happened to them.
- Get *everybody* 'on board'. Every time a new professional is engaged, the rationale has to be explained. In one case, a carer saw two traumatised victims as 'trouble makers' who were not to be trusted. Use publicity. Whilst there is a need to exercise caution, publicity can be very constructive in informing attitudes and promoting learning. Remember that this is child abuse. On occasions, there is a need to shout about the fact that older men are having sexual relationships with young children. If a 23-year-old man is having sex with a 14-year-old girl, it is not a loving relationship – it is child sexual abuse.
- It is not acceptable. The sense of outrage that professionals feel when the true facts are disclosed needs to be shared with others.
- Children need protection. However difficult they may be, and however challenging their behaviour, children under 18 years of age have a right to be protected.
- Professionals can learn a lot from one another.

Conclusions

Children generally do not wander inadvertently into prostitution. They are a valuable commodity in a cruel and violent sex work economy. As such, they are preyed on and shown a way in and abusing adults inflict very serious harm upon vulnerable young people. Sadly, this type of criminal behaviour probably features in every major town and city. In those with a recognised vice problem, it is almost certain that young people are being abused through prostitution. What we have learned is that *the problem will not present itself on your doorstep. You have to look for it and ask the right questions*. In one county without an identified street-based vice problem, a survey of professionals identified over 30 cases of suspected child abuse through prostitution.

The problem does exist and there is something we can do to deal with it. There are always competing priorities, but for all of us, protecting children from serious harm must be at the top of the list. *Local traditional police vice squads are not the solution*. A small team of dedicated professionals from police, social service, health and voluntary organisations, however, can make a big difference. If you have such a group in your area, how can it work better? **If you do not have such a team in your area, why not?** One young woman sent a card to staff. It read:

> *I know at times I have been a real pain and I have been difficult to work with. I cannot thank you enough for the help and support you have given me. I now have a new life.*

More young women should be able to say that.

The views expressed in this chapter are those of the author and do not represent the views of West Midlands Police.

CHAPTER 7

The NSPCC 'Street Matters' Project in London

Nasima Patel and Jenny J. Pearce

Why 'Street Matters' matters to us

'Street Matters' is a support project for young women at risk of, or experiencing, sexual exploitation or prostitution in London. This chapter charts the development of the project over the last three years, identifying some of the lessons learnt from its practice and research, which have developed concurrently. Throughout the chapter, the work described refers to young women but many of the issues raised are equally relevant for work with sexually exploited young men. The comments below from two young women who have used the project give an insight into why 'Street Matters' matters to them.

> They helped me find housing when I was on the streets, gave me clothing . . . supported me . . . it's confidential . . . they give you support in a crisis.
>
> (I, aged 16).

> Street Matters has made a significant difference to me and my life. The one-to-one counselling sessions were the best thing about the project especially because I felt they were informal, and I felt comfortable and relaxed.
>
> (N, aged 15).

The chapter argues in line with guidelines from government (DoH/HO/DfEE, 2000) that young women under the age of 18, who are selling or swapping sex for money or other favours in kind, should be treated as victims of abuse rather than perpetrators of crime. It challenges the proposal that those under the age of 18 who 'persistently and voluntarily' return to selling sex can be convicted for offences related to prostitution. Case material illustrates that it is these young women who are most marginalised and alienated from welfare support. Simplistic responses, for example cautions, fines or prison sentences, do nothing to address their history of loss and abuse. The chapter also proposes that practice agencies should refrain from referring to young women under 16 years old as 'prostitutes', arguing that as they are under the age of consent, they cannot be active agents working in the sex industry. As such, more effort should be placed on protecting young women who are at risk of, or experiencing sexual exploitation through co-ordinated multi-agency work and specialist project provision. Definitions of sexual exploitation are provided below, one from a young woman and the other from the '*Street Matters*' project.

Sexual exploitation
It's someone taking a part of you.

(L, aged 14).

Any activity containing or suggesting a sexual component that a person is not consenting to freely, that it contains varying degrees of coercion that could vary from gentle persuasion to intimidation or violence.

(NSPCC Street Matters Project).

Some of the issues outlined below explore the implications of enacting this approach in more detail. A specific theme is the need for a dual approach: concentrating on supporting the young woman while gathering evidence against the abuser.

Background to the project

The '*Street Matters*' project was initiated by the NSPCC between 1997–1999. From the outset, the project included a research component. Drawing on a partnership agreement between the NSPCC and Middlesex University, funding was secured through The Joseph Rowntree Foundation and Middlesex University to enquire into young women's own accounts of the choices and opportunities available to them as they progressed to adulthood. The development of the research and the project service delivery took place simultaneously, one informing the other to the culmination of findings outlined later in this discussion.

The London borough where the project is located has a visible 'red light' scene, with a history of street-based prostitution extending back over 200 years. A tourist industry has thrived in the area by making past and current activities within the sex industry a spectacle for voyeurism and intrigue. The irony of this is not lost on those women still working these streets as the tourism survives from the notion that prostitution is something apart from 'normal' life. As it is never our husbands, fathers or brothers who buy sex, so too it is 'never our mother, our daughter, or our sister but some anonymous other who is infinitely more desperate than those we love' who sell it (McKeganey and Barnard, 1996: 1).

Within the borough, youth workers had anecdotal evidence that young women were involved in activities relating to prostitution. These reports were linked to concern about young people's increasing drug use in the area, of truancy from school, of poverty and social exclusion of large sections of the local communities (London Borough, 1994; Pearce and Stanko, 2000). There were reports that young Asian women were selling sex, and the problems experienced by both adult sex workers and young people on the street were being compounded by vigilante attacks which focused on clearing the streets of prostitution. Much of this activity came from the local Bangladeshi community and had a very strong Islamic perspective to it. In response to these issues, council officers and the borough social services department met with the NSPCC in a concerted effort to develop appropriate services for supporting young women at risk of, or involved with, prostitution in the local area.

NSPCC Street Matters: staffing expertise and resources

The NSPCC '*Street Matters*' project started with a full time co-ordinator in 1999 and originally modelled it's work around street-based prostitution, building a strong detached outreach element to engage young people. A full time research officer was appointed in February 2000 to work alongside the project and undertake case study work with young women referred or contacted through outreach. The case study work provided a context within which young women could express their own views about their needs and circumstances.

The project worked to a multi-agency steering group where the social service department played a key role. Becoming increasingly aware of the demands presented by the young women, extra staffing was sought. The project received some financial support from social services' *Quality Protects* and some additional NSPCC funding. Comic Relief expressed an interest in funding what it described as a 'gritty project'. Within eight months, money for additional 1.6 posts had been raised.

The professional background of staff was of local authority social work and youth work. The researcher attached to '*Street Matters*', employed by Middlesex University, came with experience of interviewing women selling sex on the street and working with associated sexual health problems. The team shared a passion for developing appropriate services for adolescent young women – a driving force for the development of the work to date. As the work has developed, the staffing levels have remained consistent, placing pressures on staff to prioritise provision. The pressures from the work in this field can be intense (Melrose, 2002) and it was necessary to allocate time for staff support, supervision and training to enable the work to progress. While it has been difficult to prioritise this over other demands, it has been essential in retaining staff energy and commitment.

Street Matters and local support

Within the borough, there was support for the development of this service from local practitioners, many of whom were represented on the steering group. One of the key supporters was the deputy manager at one of the children's homes who was concerned that young people in care may be being exploited through prostitution. Important contacts were made with the manager of a sexual health service for young people and a child protection nurse from the local hospital. Interestingly, it was the A & E Department who had contacted the NSPCC saying they were concerned about á number of young women coming in with injuries late at night, the implication being that they were involved in sex work. Joint work from this point has been successful and productive, a somewhat unexpected outcome as it was thought that links with street-based crisis work and sexual health practice would be more forthcoming than centrally based hospital services.

Confidentiality

As the project was concerned with engaging disaffected young women, the nature of confidentiality arose as a central question. In the first year of the project's development, a lot of time was spent talking about how to engage the young women in ways that would secure their trust. Issues of confidentiality were central to these debates. There was concern that the concept of 'significant harm' proposed under the Children Act 1989 would provide too high a threshold for breaching confidentiality and therefore could lead to us losing the young person's trust in the early stages of the relationship. The project work, along with findings from previous studies (Barrett, 1997), suggested that young people would be hard to engage without a reassurance that confidentiality would be maintained. Our own child protection backgrounds acknowledged that many young people who have been abused, committed offences or continued to be hard to reach, would be frightened of what might happen after a well kept secret was disclosed. In these situations, the young person may resist support offered, responding only to a trusting relationship where they felt safe that their disclosure would be managed to protect them from harm. Struggling with these contradictions, project staff spent a lot of time defining what the thresholds for breaching confidentiality would be. Within the NSPCC there were other people doing work around what was called 'child friendly child protection systems'. This has a very strong element of advocacy and empowerment for young people and has been helpful to the development of the '*Street Matters*' project.

It was agreed that '*Street Matters*' operate a high-risk confidentiality policy. Staff would not breach confidentiality unless the young person was deemed to be in 'immediate' or 'great' danger. This policy is supported by a risk assessment matrix. It is used every time a worker feels they carry a high level of risk through maintaining confidentiality. The Area Child Protection Committee associated with the project was asked to agree the use of this policy. They agreed that, under particular circumstances, the child care system can be based on a lower threshold for breaching children's confidentiality than specified by The Children Act 1989.

Putting the policy into practice has raised important issues for the development of the service. Firstly, it has become common practice for project staff to develop intimate relationships with the young women and, nine times out of ten, permission is given to share information simply because the young people like and trust project staff. The more work has been done, the more project staff have begun to realise that the confidentiality policy depends not so much on what the young women are prepared to say, but more upon their knowledge, or definition, of the 'truth'. Sometimes, experience has shown that the young person has distorted or confused observations of their situation. We also found that, as the young women are invariably in crisis, they do not have the time or motivation to have long discussions with staff about what they perceive to be their confidentiality. Instead, they want the trust that they are developing with project staff to continue, with support and resources to meet their immediate needs. Under these circumstances, the project worker, rather than the young woman, decides how much information should be shared. As the central aim is to work with the young women to advocate for the best service to meet their needs, it is project staff who decides what to tell outside agencies. Sometimes this leaves staff feeling uncomfortable, particularly if sharing information leads to actions or interventions about which project staff feel critical.

Carrying a high-risk confidentiality policy has a direct impact on practitioners. Unless there is a clear system for sharing information and support, workers can feel that they are managing a massive deal of risk. The worry is that if the wrong judgement is made, both the young woman and working relationships with other agencies may suffer. To work with this, risk assessments are made through regular practice discussions about confidentiality within the ethos of working together with other agencies for the best interests of the child.

The methods of work are discussed in more detail before moving to discuss the client base as understood by both project work and its associated research.

Street Matters: methods of working with young women

'*Street Matters*' share premises with other NSPCC youth and community work projects operating within the borough. It offers a five-day week, 9 a.m. to

5 p.m. service, with a drop-in session one night a week continuing into the evening. Recognising that some young women will need flexible hours of contact for individual work, the project offers flexibility around time. Maintaining flexibility to meet requests for immediate support has been an effective way of engaging hard to reach young people who need you there at a point of crisis. However, operating flexible time boundaries can drain staff resources, as competing priorities have to come under regular review. To manage this, the project staff has ensured consistency of provision through three discrete methods of working.

Keywork

This is intensive, ongoing, individual work with young women. The key worker adheres to a child centred model, working at the pace and intensity set by the young woman, starting the work from 'where the young person is at'. The keywork system is based on traditional social work casework where a worker engages with the young person to establish common goals and uses the engagement process to gain confidence and trust at a deeper level in the work.

Some young people have had keywork for over two years now. Other young people have received intensive work over a period of crisis and then moved on, wanting no further contact with the project. The system offers examples of positive relationships for the young woman, countering previous experiences that relationships with adults are abusive or unreliable. It provides a listening and advocacy service and a 'safe place' for young women to begin to challenge destructive elements of their own and others' behaviour. The level of need presented by different young women is high as young women face multi-faceted problems. Young women's well being fluctuates depending upon levels of substance misuse, changing circumstances at home, or in care, and upon the actions of others – usually, abusive and violent men. Project staff will see a young woman making progress, establishing benefits and then all this can disappear for reasons that only become apparent later after intensive, supportive keywork. Staff work with feelings of exhaustion, frustration and anger on a daily basis and this can be overwhelming.

The young women can be classified as 'high maintenance', needing extra support as statutory services are invariably able to offer only cursory services to them. To sustain this level of support through keywork, staff supervision becomes a key component. It is easy for staff to feel burdened, feeling solely responsible for the young women. Supervision provides the context for these burdens to be shared. The management of large workloads, within a small staff team, has often made keywork difficult to maintain. However, it is one of the central components of project work and has developed as an important model.

Drop-in

The drop-in facility is available as an 'open group' for one night each week. Young women can 'drop-in' to get support and advice alongside provisions such as food, condoms and washing facilities, including use of a washing machine and dryer. Providing a meal has been an important component to the work – young women enjoying the chance to cook and to eat together. For some, it may be one of the few hot meals eaten during the week. The drop-in has been one of the most successful areas of the project's work. It has proved to be an effective way of introducing new young people to the project, especially if they have not wanted a key worker, or staff shortages meant that keywork was not possible at that time.

The drop-in is based on a centre based youth work model with child centred activities. Activities follow a six to eight week programme. These have included workshops on topics such as 'drugs', 'sexual relationships' and activities such as ice skating and going to the cinema. There is a strong emphasis on peer support and group work, young women being involved in organising and running the drop-in sessions themselves. This approach has led to one young woman attending a 'peer education course' with the intention of returning to assist in extending drop-in provision to the younger age group within the project.

The drop-in does not suit all the young women. Most that use the facility are black and Asian, providing indirect support for each other on issues such as the relationship between sexual exploitation, racism and culture. The support is indirect as the topics are rarely discussed in a formal and supervised way. Although white young women are actively included, the snowballing effect, where young women bring their friends, has meant that the drop-in is used predominantly by Black African Caribbean and Asian girls who have built a support base amongst themselves. The facility reveals, as found by the research, that most sexually exploited young women of Asian origin will experience exploitation behind closed doors, away from the view of statutory or voluntary agencies. For these young women the drop-in facility is often their only contact with practitioners who are able to offer support. The drop-in has not suited many of the over 17s who have felt bored with the programme selected by the majority of those in their mid-teens. Similarly, younger women aged 12 and 13 have demonstrated interest in isolated trips rather than the full programme. The aims, objectives and target groups of the drop-in are under continual review with the young women and plans are afoot to establish a drop-in for the younger group.

In the first year of the drop-in, both staff and young people struggled around establishing ground rules for acceptable behaviour. The balance between being informal enough to engage while maintaining basic rules for safety purposes was difficult to gauge. With time, a few ground rules have been agreed. For example, it was agreed that mobile phones should only receive emergency calls during workshop activities. Often calls would be from boyfriends or dealers and would upset the flow of the activities. It was also agreed that young women would not interrupt each other when talking in a workshop or discussion group, placing equal priority on listening as on talking.

Outreach

Outreach work undertaken by the project is twofold providing street-based outreach and outreach of the service into joint work with other professionals such as schools and social work.

Street-based outreach

Between December 2000 and March 2001, '*Street Matters*' undertook weekly outreach in the local 'red light area'. This drew on detached, street-based models for working – project staff going out in a car, 'hanging around' specific areas to gain the trust of young women, offering advice on children's rights, legal concerns, sexual health, harm minimisation and other issues.

In 2001, this outreach was suspended for two reasons. Firstly, it was difficult to sustain due to limited staffing. Each outreach session took place with a minimum of three staff. This made it difficult to maintain outreach alongside keywork and drop-in. Secondly, the project was receiving an increasing number of referrals of young women from professionals, drawing heavily on staff time for keywork and drop-in activities. This decision was also taken because a local drug prevention project was conducting regular outreach in the area, providing similar services to '*Street Matters*' outreach.

This decision effectively meant turning away from street-based prostitution to working with sexually exploited young women who were engaged in swapping or selling sex from 'behind closed doors'. It also meant that young women from different racial and cultural backgrounds were accommodated by the service. As the research outlined below shows, it is mainly white young women who are located selling sex on the street.

The decision provoked consideration of the relationship between prostitution, sexual exploitation and location. The sexually exploited young women worked with through referrals and drop-in did not necessarily conform to the popular stereotype of 'street-based' prostitution. Rather, experience demonstrated that sexual exploitation may be experienced by a range of young women in a variety of locations. Many of the young women worked with may have been exchanging sex for favours but not self-defining as working in prostitution. It was important to remain open to the different definitions presented by the young women and, while maintaining some street-based outreach, ensuring that access was maintained with those whose exploitation is more hidden.

Working together: reaching out to work in schools with other professionals
Working closely with statutory and voluntary agencies has been critical to project development. The partnership arrangement with Middlesex University provided a platform for sharing expertise that was helpful in the early stages when fundraising was crucial. It became evident during the early stages that an ethos of 'working together' between professionals could help to keep an optimistic framework around service development. *'Street Matters'* regularly works with voluntary and statutory agencies to share expertise and co-ordinate limited resources for the welfare of the child. An example of this is given below, with an outline of some of the complexities that can emerge through joint work.

Work with schools
The project work and associated research has shown that schools have an important role in identifying and working with early stages of sexual exploitation. Project work in schools has taken place in two forms.

Firstly, project workers have worked alongside school teaching staff to include 'sexual exploitation' as part of any sex education or personal and social development component of the curriculum. Questions such as 'How can you tell if an older boyfriend may become abusive?' 'What is an appropriate age group for children to hang around with?' 'How can drug use make you vulnerable to abuse from adults?' have been covered as generic topics for discussion by those participating.

Secondly, specialist 'closed' groups have been run with young women within schools. This has been done as joint work with social work. For example, one school was concerned that a small group of girls was leaving the school during lunch break, getting into cars with men and returning before school closing time or not at all. The school was keen to work with the young women on this behaviour by offering them an opportunity to discuss what was taking place. It was agreed that *'Street Matters'* would run a specialist group in conjunction with the social service department, and that the group would be closed for the particular girls concerned.

This joint work has raised a number of interesting questions – one being about the need to gain parental consent before the young women could take part in such a group. The social services department felt adamant that parental consent should be sought. The school voiced ambivalence, wanting to adopt as flexible an approach as possible. The *'Street Matters'* team drew on 'Gillick Competence' to argue that, under agreed circumstances; parental consent was not needed (Gillick, 1996 in Powell, 2001). The concerns of '*Street Matters*' staff were that the young women's behaviour could result from existing abuse or violence at home. If so, the situation experienced by the girls might be made more difficult if the parent or carer were to be informed of her attendance at the group. If this were the case, the opportunity to facilitate an environment where the young women could begin to discuss their behaviour may have been lost. Following extensive discussion it was agreed that parental consent should be sought for the young women to attend the group. However, the explicit nature of the group and the issues that it was designed to address remained covert. The rationale for this action was explained to the young women. This proved a successful way of engaging the young women in looking at their activities during the lunch breaks *and* at their feelings about what could or could not be discussed with their parents or carers. The specialist 'closed group work' resulted in the young women addressing the risks that they were taking by leaving school during the lunch break to go off with older men.

It transpired from the outreach work with schools and social work that a resource gap exists as school staff inevitably have to focus on the overall well being of all their pupils, and social services departments have a duty to focus on the wider responsibility of working with families. The joint work through outreach services in different professional locations meant that '*Street Matters*' staff could help access and then advocate for the young women's views. For this to be successful, open and regular dialogue between project staff, the school and social work staff must be maintained.

The client profile: project work and associated research findings

As noted above, a partnership arrangement with Middlesex University ensured that research could take place alongside project development. Funded by The Joseph Rowntree Foundation and Middlesex University, the research aimed to explore young women's perspectives about the choices and opportunities available to them. It was developed in two NSPCC projects, in '*Street Matters*' in London and through a youth work project in a northern city. For the project, this meant that research was conducted without undue demand on staff time and that an 'outside' perspective on the work was provided. For the research staff, the project provided a point for contact with young women and a reference for professional consultation on ethical issues such as confidentiality and safety. It also provided a base to which young women contacted through the research could be referred for follow up work.

Street Matter's project client group data

The project had ongoing contact with 77 young women between July 1999 and April 2002. 27 young women were contacted through outreach, 26 were referred by other agencies and 24 self-referred for one-to-one work after hearing about the project from friends or visiting the drop-in. It was invariably difficult to ascertain the age of those encountered on outreach (27). Many of the young women avoided talking of their age while others gave their age as older than they looked. One girl, known to local services had just turned 16 in 2001. The remainder were aged between 16 and 21.

Table 1 below shows the age range of the remaining 50 young women at the point of contact and Table 2 their ethnic origin.

Table 1: Age of the 50 young women worked with through drop-in or keywork provision July 1999–April 2002 (this data excludes the 27 young women met on outreach)

Age	Number of young women
13	3
14	7
15	16
16	12
17	9
18–20	3

Table 2: Racial origin of the 77 young women

White UK	36
Bangladeshi	20
Black African/Caribbean	10
Mixed race: Black AC and white	6
European	1
Mixed race European/UK	4

27 of the 36 white young women were met through the outreach provision. Keywork has taken place with 50 young women, all of whom had used the drop-in at some point, 26 of whom used it regularly within their weekly routines. The project database has been enhanced by the work of the research, the findings of which are outlined below.

Research findings

The research drew on findings from case study work undertaken with a total of 55 young women aged 18 and under; 25 were from a northern city and 30 from London (Pearce et al., 2003). The young women were at risk or currently being exploited through prostitution. The work aimed to provide young women's own accounts of the choices and opportunities available to them in their transition to adulthood. It used a range of individual casework methods and other exercises. Table 3 shows the age of the young women who took part in the research.

Table 3: Age of young women (n = 55)

Age	Number of young women
13	3
14	13
15	6
16	13
17	14
18	6

Multi-faceted problems

Table 4 shows the numbers of young women from each location against the particular problems they were facing.

In line with existing research, Table 4 shows that the most common problems experienced by the young women were truanting from school or school exclusion, substance misuse, histories of familial physical and sexual abuse, abusive relationships with violent men and sexual health problems. The young women faced a number of problems, most dealing with between 10 and 17 issues at any one time. These problems were invariably inter-linked, meaning that effective service delivery needed to work with multi-faceted problems of, for example, current and previous experiences of violence, substance misuse, running away careers and self-harming behaviour. A central theme presented by the young women was their experiences of violent and abusive relationships with older men.

39 of the 55 young women were in violent relationships with boyfriends. L, aged 17, talked of the pain caused by having had a chilli paste rubbed into her 'private parts', saying that she didn't 'want to remember. It just hurt'. The physical and emotional pain caused by such attacks remained with the young women who needed intensive support by project workers to begin to speak about the impact it had had on their lives.

Table 4: Issues identified by the 55 young women's case studies

	London (n = 30)	Northern City (n = 25)	Total (n = 55)
History of intermittent truanting	30	25	55
Regular (at least weekly) misuse of alcohol	30	25	55
History of going missing from home/running away	28	25	53
History of familial physical abuse	27	20	47
School non-attender (Not on a school role)	24	18	42
Sexual health problems	27	23	40
Boyfriend who is physically violent	19	20	39
Has been in care or accommodated by the local authority	21	18	39
Boyfriend at least 4 years older than themselves (most aged 25-35)	18	18	36
Self-harms	18	16	34
Regular (at least weekly) heroin misuse	15	15	30
Bullied at school	15	11	26
History of familial sexual abuse	12	13	25
Works for boyfriend (selling sex for money for boyfriend or selling/swapping for drugs for his use)	9	14	23
Has been raped	12	10	22
Police record (no offence relating to prostitution)	10	12	22
Homeless	13	9	22
Attempted suicide	11	7	18
Has been abducted (held against their will for at least two nights)	7	9	16
Abducted by a boyfriend	7	8	15
Known to have bullied others at school	6	6	12
Has been pregnant	6	3	9
Worked with police to press charges against abuser	4	3	7
Has had a baby	4	2	6
Diagnosed learning difficulties	2	1	3
Diagnosed mental health problems	2	1	3
Has been in prison	1	2	3

36 young women had boyfriends at least four years older than themselves, the average ages of boyfriends being between 20 and 30-years-old. 23 of the 36 young women were selling or swapping sex for money or drugs for their boyfriend's use. As found in previous research, the process of 'grooming' for prostitution relies upon the man making the young woman believe that he is 'in love with her', invariably doing so whilst increasing her dependence upon drugs (Green, 1992; Dodsworth, 2000). Despite the violence and abuse reported by the young women, many spoke of intense emotional attachment to the boyfriend, only six calling the boyfriend a pimp.

Categories of risk

Analysis of the nature of the problems when compared against the age range and personal circumstances illustrated by the young women's case studies has suggested three categories of 'risk'. These are described below in Table 5:

Table 5: Categories of risk

Category 1: At risk
Running away from home or care, with prolonged periods of truanting from school and going missing. Beginning to engage in emotional and sexual relationships with older, abusive men.

Category 2: Swapping sex
As with Category 1 but with increasing engagement in intense sexual and emotional relationships with older violent men, with increasing misuse of alcohol and drugs, swapping sex for affection, money, drugs, accommodation or other returns 'in kind'.

Category 3: Selling sex
Spending extended periods of time on the street, living in temporary accommodations or being homeless, selling sex and intermittently identifying as working in 'prostitution'.

The idea of placing the young women into one of three categories emerged during the research. This classification was not, however, fully enacted until the final analysis, which illustrated distinct stages of vulnerability and exposure to sexual exploitation. Analysis of the age range of young women within each of the categories shows how movement from Category 1 to Category 3 takes place with age. While young women from different age groups are found in most of the three categories, it is evident that all those in Category 3, selling sex, are aged 16 and over. As noted earlier, all young women in Category 3 from London were white. There was one dual heritage white/African Caribbean young woman met on outreach in the northern city. Apart from this, all the young women who worked on the street were white.

Table 6 below shows the ages of the young women against the risk categories to which they have been assigned.

Table 6: Categories 1 to 3 by age

Age	Category 1 At risk (n = 19)		Category 2 Swapping sex (n = 15)		Category 3 Selling sex (n = 21)	
13	3	100%	0	0%	0	0%
14	7	54%	6	46%	0	0%
15	3	50%	3	50%	0	0%
16	4	31%	2	15%	7	54%
17	2	14%	3	21%	9	64%
18			1	17%	5	83%

Many of the problems identified in Table 4 (above) exist for young women in each of the categories. For example, there is little variation between Categories 1 to 3 of young women's histories of previous sexual and physical abuse, experiences of having been 'looked after' by the local authority, of self-harming and attempting suicide, or of having been raped or abducted. The movement into and between the categories was influenced by recent experiences of emotional, physical or sexual abuse, either from family or care circumstances or from older 'boyfriends'. It was also affected by the young women's capacity to employ coping mechanisms, themselves influenced by substance misuse which, in turn, had varying influence on their lives.

Although young women experienced many of the same sorts of problems, young women in Category 3 faced additional problems. Although all young women from each of the categories had histories of running away from home, the length of time away from home often increased with each run, making the young woman more vulnerable to risk. The longer the time spent on the street, the more vulnerable the young women were to shifting from Category 1 (at risk of being sexually exploited) to Category 2 (swapping sex for accommodation or drugs). Young women in Category 3 were more likely to be homeless, to have a criminal record, and to have severe problems with substance misuse, particularly heroin. Five young women in Category 1 were regular heroin users compared to six in Category 2, and 19 in Category 3.

Despite this escalation in the range of problems experienced, the number of young women who reported (or whose casework noted) contact with social services throughout the 18 months in which the research took place, was lower for those in Category 3, than in Category 1. 18 of the 19 in Category 1 had contact with social services, 13 of the 15 in Category 2, and 10 of the 21 in Category 3. It may be expected that as most of those in Category 1 were younger, they may be more likely to be in touch with social services, and that it is the 'older' girls on the street who are more difficult to engage.

Thematic considerations

Using the categories described above, the project and the local ACPC have begun to look at the development of targeted, fast-track services to meet the needs of individual young women. It is recognised that project based key-work and preventative work in schools will be most applicable for girls in Category 1, whilst those in Category 2 may benefit from drop-in facilities supported by access to specialist foster carers and drug and alcohol harm minimisation programmes. Street-based outreach services could likewise be developed to enhance appropriate provision for those placed in Category 3. While all of these services could be applicable for any young woman at any time, the research and project work have together tried to establish target groups with particular fast-track services applicable to their needs.

Two other considerations arose from analysis of the qualitative data. Firstly, case studies demonstrated that the times that the young women were most in need were often the times that they had rejected support. To counter this, the concept of **therapeutic outreach** has been developed. It means that when a worker continues to reach out if a young woman has gone missing or has rejected an offer of support, this can be therapeutic in itself. Therapeutic outreach recognises that for hard to reach young people, workers have to be prepared to put in three quarters effort for a quarter return.

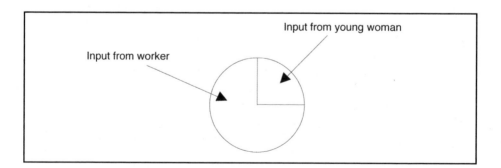

Therapeutic outreach

The second theme that arose from analysis of research findings was that project work was invariably working with young women who, if adults, would be perceived to be in situations of domestic violence. Invariably the young woman was acting *as if* she were an adult. She was aware that her boyfriend was abusing her yet was also aware that he was dependant upon her at various practical and emotional levels. Child protection frameworks did not seem adequately to address these complexities or to recognise the extent to which young women saw themselves as 'in love' with their abusive boyfriends (pimps). On the other hand, domestic violence discourses provided a framework for understanding and responding. To retain a focus on the needs of the young person as a child, whilst recognising the complexity of the emotional and practical relationship they were in, both child protection *and* domestic violence policies and practices are being incorporated within project work.

Conclusion

'*Street Matters*' has become a central focus for providing support to some of the most disaffected young women either at risk of, or involved with, sexual exploitation. Some young women have stayed in touch with the project – 12 for over a year, attending both drop-in and keywork.

Working together with outside agencies, the project is working to improve services for the client group. For example:

- It is a part of a wider consortium in London – *Somewhere Safe* – primarily set up to look at the issue of appropriate accommodation for this client group.
- It is looking to explore the option of working with and providing training for specialist foster carers to provide respite, temporary accommodation for the young women as well as having more hostels for young people (16–18 years).

As the work has developed, the project increasingly finds that sexual exploitation is not the main focus of involvement with young people. Advice on relationships, risk taking and drug misuse provides a base line constant, while increasing amounts of time are spent supporting young women to find appropriate housing and deal with the impact of low self-esteem, isolation and poverty.

Our experience has shown that while many young women may present as chaotic and confused, this is often because they are experiencing their teenage years coming from disrupted, often abusive, backgrounds. However, it is often the case that the presenting distress is not only to do with the past abuse or exploitation but also to do with frustration and anger at being unable to receive the sustained support they need. '*Street Matters*' is part of a drive to reveal the complex nature of these needs and to expand supported well-resourced provision for the young women concerned.

CHAPTER 8

Terrence Higgins Trust West Street Team: Working with Young Men

Tim Darch

Introduction

Generally, society finds it hard to deal with the problem of prostitution. When the problem of young men involved in prostitution is raised, most people will deny that it exists. Until every local authority, health authority and police force acknowledges their existence, and begins to address their basic needs, they will have failed in their duty of care for some of the most vulnerable young men in our society today.

Background to the project

In mid-1997 Terrence Higgins Trust West (formally the Aled Richards Trust) carried out an environmental scan of male sex work in Bristol. The environmental scan took the form of a short needs assessment of those clients willing to be interviewed, and was carried out following a major police operation against abusers of young men and boys. The primary objective of the scan was to discover what services and support young men selling sex needed to exit the sex trade. The report made several recommendations for working with these highly vulnerable young men.

Some of the findings at the time pointed to a need for the Terrence Higgins Trust West's Gay Men's Project to work with Freedom Youth (a Bristol based youth group for lesbian, gay, bisexual and transgender young people and for those who are questioning their sexuality) to include issues of exploitation in relationships and sex work, in their social education agenda. It was also recommended that there should be information specifically for male sex workers in the leaflet racks in gay venues, and that the Terrence Higgins Trust West should provide relevant services with information, resources, training and assistance with working with young men who sell sex.

It was felt that due to the nature of the client group and the work being undertaken, the Terrence Higgins Trust West Gay Men's Health Project should take the 'lead agency' role in Bristol in relation to young men who sell sex. This was considered to be especially important as the Gay Men's Project acknowledged that male sex workers are part of its work but at the time could not ensure that appropriate services (i.e. safer sex information, condoms and lubricant, etc.) were available, due to lack of funding.

In April 2000, the Aled Richards Trust merged with Terrence Higgins Trust, to form Terrence Higgins Trust West. Within two months, very limited exploratory work was initiated, with the purpose of further identifying the needs of young men who sell sex. This pilot scheme operated from early June until December 2000, and made contact with 17 young men selling sex. Of the 17 interviewed it was found that all worked 'on street' selling sex and were mostly homeless, some had been through the care system, some had issues around their sexuality and most had drug dependencies. All the findings of the original scan were more evident at the time of this second exercise and it was obvious that addressing one issue in isolation would not address the imbalance in a young person's life. It was therefore decided that a 'holistic' approach was needed, which should include appropriate support and advocacy work.

Many of the men who cruised the sites, (sought consensual free sex between each other) within any given three-month period, had either bought or had been paid for sex. This demonstrated that the boundaries between sex workers, punters, and cruisers were very blurred and therefore sessional work must extend to cruisers and punters as a secondary target group. A major concern was in relation to the number of 'opportunistic' sex workers, which was much higher than first envisaged – these included students, those on benefits, and those who needed to supplement any form of income to purchase drugs, irrespective of their sexuality. It was suggested that these people should also be informed about the services available. As it appeared that the number of opportunistic sex workers increased during certain times of the year, it was decided that extra sessions would be arranged to cover them.

Many of the young men who remained involved in sex work had a strong distrust of any form of authority. As a result, they were not reporting any form of crime committed against them. A strategy was therefore developed to enable a high level of trust to be built and by doing so, offer encouragement to the young men to report these crimes, and offer support to the individuals concerned. Following police advice, we agreed that any crime that we were told about would be reported anonymously. We also found that a large number of sex workers, cruisers, and punters had been the victims of homophobic 'hate crimes', but they chose not to report them. Again, ways to report these were devised. This included offering facilitation for the victim to report these crimes. Should a person wish to remain anonymous then we would be able to report these crimes, with their consent, anonymously to the police.

A number of young men involved in selling sex and cruisers were identified as appearing to be underage. It had been agreed with social services that when contact with someone who appeared to be underage was made, we would encourage these people to seek alternative and safer forms of contact. We would, for example, refer them to Freedom Youth provided they met the following criteria:

- They were not persistent.
- They self-identified as being gay, bisexual or were questioning their sexuality.
- They were seeking peer support.

This policy was agreed because many young men can become isolated when exploring their sexuality and it is therefore important to ensure that they meet with appropriate peer groups. It was agreed that in these circumstances we would provide support and advice but not refer them to social services or child protection. It was also agreed, however, that we would take immediate reporting action if they disclosed abuse, were persistent in returning to the locations, or appeared to be at any risk in relation to their well being and safety.

We always assess the apparent maturity of any young man we come into contact with. If we have any concerns about their ability to understand the issues surrounding risk behaviour, we would have no hesitation in invoking the necessary statutory child protection measures. If we considered that a young man under 16 years of age was at risk (other than described above), we would always call for an emergency case review as required by Bristol Social Services Child Protection Procedures. During the period in which the project has been working, we have not encountered any difficulties with these procedures.

Initially, the client groups viewed the street team workers with great suspicion. Over a period of months, however, levels of trust increased dramatically even to the extent that some young men were happy to share real names, real personal problems and talk openly about both major and minor issues affecting their lives. In January 2001, funding was secured from the Home Office, and work with young men up to 21-years-old was extended through the Pandora Project.

Methodology of the project

The Pandora Project is a multi-agency partnership aimed at addressing the problems faced by young people male and female involved in prostitution. Partner agencies in Bristol include, Bristol Drugs Project, Barnardo's Against Sexual Abuse, Social Services, United Bristol Health Care Trust Sexual Health Services, Avon and Somerset Constabulary and Bristol City Council. To ensure that the Terrence Higgins Trust West was able to provide the best possible service to clients, a formal structure was adopted with clearly defined roles for project members. This ensured that all people working on the project had immediate and fully defined procedures in place to protect the clients as well as themselves.

Sessional staff

The sessional workers, who have direct contact with clients, ensure that they deal with the immediate issues that the young person presents. These issues range from being homeless through to support over contracting a sexual infection. The workers provide advice and support on issues such as homelessness and accessible housing solutions. In addition, they offer encouragement to the young people to change their lifestyles by taking control of issues affecting them. These issues range from safer sex methods, through to reducing crimes committed by them to gain money for drugs. Workers also assist the young men in determining appropriate methods for reducing drug dependencies. Where necessary, they carry out one to one support work with young men entering into detox and ensure continuity of support before, during, and after detox.

Members of the team also offer young men support in reporting crimes committed against them and provide encouragement to report witnessed crimes. In addition, individuals who may be the perpetrators of crime are encouraged to desist from their current activities. The young men are additionally provided with impartial advice on sexual health including the opportunity to be tested and receive free hepatitis vaccinations. As a matter of course, workers provided free condoms and lubricants and correct advice on usage. Most importantly, the workers offer a confidential listening ear which is non-judgemental and non-discriminatory. This enables the young men to discuss personal issues and is probably one of the most important facets of the work. It allows the workers to continue to gain trust amongst sex workers, punters and cruisers and means that the clients feel they can talk about personal issues and are supported appropriately in dealing with them.

Management

The primary role of the manager was to ensure that all procedures were adhered to and that all follow up work that was needed or promised to a client was carried out. Where advocacy work was required, he also ensured that the appropriate persons were tasked to undertake the work. The manager was responsible for maintaining budgets and ensuring that where training was required by the sessional workers it was obtained in a timely and cost effective manner. He was required to deal with issues that required more in depth work than could be offered initially on the street and ensured that other organisations followed up on referrals as required.

The clients

When the work of the Pandora Project began, it soon became clear that the scale of the problem had been seriously underestimated. Originally, we had thought we might come into contact with approximately 10–12 young men selling sex throughout the first year. What was totally unexpected was the **46** contacts made with male sex workers in the first three months. This trend continued throughout the year resulting in 87 contacts in the first 12 months. The majority of contacts (98 per cent) were White and English. We have no doubt, however, that should we be able to access ethnic minority groups (whose involvement in sex work tends to be more hidden), there would potentially be the same sort of numbers there.

Most of the young men we contacted had been in care at some stage in their lives (90 per cent). A vast majority felt that they had been unable to discuss issues around sexuality with the care staff and therefore tended to feel that they had been 'failed' by the social care system. They felt the main problem was that if they talked about these issues, the social worker would 'turn' against them. Although these fears proved to be mostly unfounded, we are aware of some social workers who appear not to understand issues relating to sexual difference.

Some young men had remained in the care system until they were 18, and on leaving care, felt that they had 'failed in life'. In reality of course, they had been *failed by* various social institutions, resulting in them now selling sex. Only one young man with whom we work is not homeless and the vast majority live in various homeless hostels in Bristol. Others live with punters. Although this is far from ideal, they prefer this to the hostel environment.

What was pleasing was the low numbers of under 16s encountered during the project. As explained above, we had agreed that no formal child protection reporting action would be taken if these contacts satisfied certain criteria. Each contact made that fitted these criteria was referred to Freedom Youth. As a result, these young men were able to enter a supportive peer group, and ceased to frequent the known areas used by the other young men involved in selling sex. What certainly did come as a surprise was that older male sex workers informed us of the presence of anyone under 16 and we were therefore able to access them very quickly.

Many of the young men had numerous problems that could not be tackled in isolation, such as drug dependency and homelessness. We therefore decided to work with each young man as appropriate, from initial contact right through to complete exit from prostitution. This approach has been shown to be highly effective. On more than one occasion a young man who has been dealing with multiple issues has warmed to us as they found they only needed to tell their life history once.

We quickly identified seven principle issues that needed to be addressed on a holistic basis:

- Social exclusion (we treat this as an issue, as the young men regard this exclusion from society as being a separate problem. It could, however, be appropriately regarded as consisting of a combination of the following elements).
- Drug and alcohol issues.
- Crime and crime reduction.
- Sexual health.
- Homelessness.
- Personal rights of the individual young man, in as much as they are entitled to the same rights as any other person.
- Legal issues, which may need to be dealt with due to any possible action against them i.e. persistent soliciting, theft, etc.

In general, each young man would be confronting at least five of these issues. Many had given up trying to resolve these problems themselves due to previous set backs they had experienced. Because different agencies are responsible for delivering services to meet these various needs, these issues tend to be tackled in isolation rather than holistically. The problems these young people face are so often interconnected, it is obvious that they require a 'joined-up' response.

Although we offer effective and suitable choices for these young men to work with other agencies, generally they seem to prefer to work with us. This appears to be for two reasons. Firstly, many are ashamed of the nature of the activity in which they are involved and, secondly, many have issues in relation to their sexuality, which they do not wish to discuss with others. Many have previously accessed other services, but have chosen to break this contact. Some were frightened that should they become known as male prostitutes, then many of the agencies would refuse to work with them. Although these fears proved to be completely unfounded, they nevertheless prevented many of the young men from accessing appropriate services to deal with their problems. This was also, in part, due to the highly chaotic lifestyles many were leading. This meant that some had failed to maintain contact with agencies, or had been requested to come back when they had more determination to succeed.

As we continued our work, there seemed to be a change in the clients' attitudes towards us. Although they had come to trust us and wanted to work with us, we had neither the funding nor time available to work with all at once. This led to a distancing between some of the clients and us; consequently, we had to decide with whom we were going to work on a priority basis. It is hard to decide who is most vulnerable, but we try to assess each young man and undertake a risk assessment of his probability of accepting help from us.

Unfortunately, that does sometimes mean that young men who are most at risk do not always get the help they need at the time. It is a hard truth, but it is better to work with two young men who can be helped to exit in a short time than to work with one young man who has neither the will nor the wish to exit. For us, the most pressing priority was to work with those who were most vulnerable, not just from prostitution, but also from becoming involved in other criminal activity. Unfortunately, due to a lack of resources, we are able to work closely with no more than two young men at a time. To supplement this, the sessional staff give much of their time voluntarily. One area of practice that developed with the project was continuation support. It was found that if we enabled a young man to exit and then left him to his own devices, he quickly returned to sex work. The only way that anyone can effectively enable young men to exit is to offer appropriate support from day one and then be prepared to support the individual concerned for the foreseeable future.

We estimate that on any one client, we spend approximately 200 hours working with them, of which 58 would be funded sessional work, and the remainder being voluntary. Many organisations could not sustain these voluntary hours unless there is very strong support, both from the managers and the sessional workers themselves.

Drug use

One of our biggest concerns is in relation to the numbers of young men living with drug dependencies. Almost all (98 per cent) of contacts made were using heroin or a cocktail of different class 'A' drugs.

Bristol has had problematic drug issues for many years and appears to have a disproportionately high percentage of heroin users under 25 years of age. A trend that now appears common amongst the young men is known as the 'party bag' – a mix of heroin and crack cocaine for the same price as a normal fix of heroin. There is therefore a very strong need for a coherent national strategy for dealing with class 'A' drugs.

Sexuality

Many of the young men we come into contact with initially disclose that they are heterosexual, but when we talk with them, they are actually very confused about their sexuality. When talking with the various young men we are very conscious that they must make their own minds up about their sexuality, and many are surprised to find that the sessional staff are gay. This always leads to long discussions about sexuality and what is or isn't gay or straight. Many will actually begin to look at themselves and start the often painful process of self-identification. When they have self-identified they suddenly become very easy to work with, as very often the root cause of their problems is sexuality, and the biggest hurdle is then surmounted! On the other hand, however, there are a number who are heterosexual, have girlfriends and some have babies. They have often decided to sell sex as there is less chance of ending up in prison than by resorting to other forms of crime. Although many people automatically assume that all men selling sex to men must be gay, we have found this to be true only in approximately 80 per cent of the cases. The other 20 per cent are heterosexual.

Abuse

Around 25 per cent of the clients will talk about previous abuse within the family home or care system, and many of these young men blame their current situation directly on this abuse. It is imperative that each young man's story around abuse is taken seriously, and any necessary actions are based on individual circumstances. All those who have spoken about abuse are very careful not to divulge real identities, which means it is difficult to report this as appropriate. We are at all times aware of the sensitivities surrounding the disclosure of abuse and offer all the support we can. This can range from introducing them to specialist counselling services, to more anonymous help lines. We have found, however, that they prefer to work directly with us and choose not to access other support networks.

We have agreed procedures that are invoked each time a young person declares abuse and these are the guidelines set by social services and the Area Child Protection Team. On each occasion, the limited information given has prevented any formal action being taken.

Criminal activity

Due to the nature of the activity in which the young people are involved, they are highly susceptible to crimes being committed against them. These range from homophobic verbal attacks through to rape. Many of the clients believe that the police will not believe them and, furthermore, all have a firm belief that these crimes are just a 'normal' risk of the activity in which they are involved. This was one of our priority areas to work in, to help these young men accept that this sort of crime is not acceptable, and would be taken seriously by the police. Despite all the necessary encouragement, not one young man has reported any crime against himself. One thing we have been able to put in place is that when they report a crime against them, they allow us to fill in a third party report for them, which is anonymous and very vague in nature, but at least it is a step in the right direction.

Confidentiality

When we meet with a young man involved in sex work for the first time, we are very careful to emphasise that confidentially is paramount. Very often, they will try to 'trap' the outreach workers by feeding them false information. This is done in an attempt either to test the outreach worker's integrity or to try to shock them. It is important that outreach workers do not over-react at this stage or the young men will become wary and may even refuse to have contact with the sessional staff again.

It is equally important to explain to the young men that the intention is not to stop them working but to offer them ways to leave the work when they want to. In the early stages of working with a young man, we would always tell him to leave us if a punter were there. By adopting this approach in the early stages, they quickly accept us, and more importantly begin to trust us. It is only later in the contact process that we encourage them to stay with us and talk when punters are around. It is impossible to say when this change of tact comes into effect, as it depends on each young man. In some instances, it has been within the first few sessions and in others after many months.

Once we have their attention and they do sit and talk with us, it is quite common for the young men actually to introduce us to punters. When the project started, we were not planning to work with punters, and although they are not our primary target group, we have found that some of the issues they have can be addressed – for example, informing them of other gay venues (this normally happens when we find the punter is a married man). Others may also have drug problems and we will always refer accordingly.

Why sell sex?

We are frequently asked why these young men become involved in selling sex, and we are the first to admit that there is no simple answer. There are, however, many common experiences amongst those we work with and these are described below:

- Currently, all have a drug dependency of some form. A coherent, 'on street', drugs intervention strategy therefore has to be employed to enable these young men to tackle their drug use.
- Many have issues surrounding their sexuality. This is an issue that must be dealt with using utmost care, as it is often intricately related to selling sex, being homeless and being drug dependant.
- All have some form of housing problem. There is therefore a need to deal with the problem of finding and supporting suitable accommodation.
- Most have been, or are, involved in other forms of criminal activity. There is therefore a need to offer support and advice to enable them to find alternative legal forms of income.

- All are being abused by the nature of the activity in which they are involved. Thankfully, all statutory bodies now recognise this, which makes it easier to support these young men.
- All recognise that they are at the lower end of the 'social ladder'. Most have been there so long, however, that they have difficulty accepting that change is possible. It is in this area that we are able to make the biggest impact. By helping them to see that they can start the long uphill climb, they gain the confidence necessary to make the first steps, albeit with continued ongoing support from the workers.

It is often hard to point to a single reason for them entering sex work, as the underlying factors are often intertwined. It is possible, however, to work on all areas simultaneously, so that the young men do not have to try and separate out the issues, until they are in a position to do so.

Issues still to be addressed

Over the time the project has been running, several issues have been identified that need to be addressed in order to work effectively with the young men. These are:

- A lack of direct access resources, such as suitable safe accommodation, which meets minimum standards.
- A lack of recognition of the problems they face on the part of the police, local authorities and other organisations.
- The project is a very early intervention, and only addresses the symptoms. Currently there is no work dealing with the causes of male prostitution. Until these are addressed, no project will be 100 per cent effective.
- This type of work cannot be target orientated. We are only able to offer choices to the young men and it is up to them if they choose to utilise a service we have encouraged them to use.
- There is a need to work with social services, schools and official bodies to address the problems a young person may be confronting in relation to their sexuality.
- It must be recognised that some aspects of social policy have a major negative impact on young men selling sex to men. Society does not want to accept that they are there. It is very clear from all the media coverage and all the research that there is now tacit recognition of young women who are abused through prostitution but there is still a denial around young men.
- Unfortunately, many of the crises that occur do so when we are unable to provide the support they need – that is, outside of normal working hours. Consideration therefore needs to be given to establishing some

form of crisis line that would operate 24 hours a day, seven days a week. We have found that when a young person is in crisis, they tend to be the most responsive to ideas for exit strategies.

- The project at present is only funded to work in Bristol City, but many of the young men we come into contact with live in bordering areas. Many admit that they also sell sex in these areas, and only come into Bristol occasionally. It is therefore important for projects to be regionally based, as this is the only way effectively to engage the young men in the areas from which they come.
- It is imperative that the appropriate budgetary allocation is given to each project in a multi-agency partnership. This should be based on the number of people they are working with directly, and the infrastructure of the parent organisation.
- Any project working with young men selling sex to men *must* have sustainability. It is counter-productive to work with them only over a short period (a year for example) when from the outset it is obvious that the problems they are confronting will take many years to deal with. Any project of this nature, if only working on a short-term basis, will only hinder these young men, as they will just see it as another agency that has ultimately let them down.

Three statements come to mind when trying to say how to work effectively with these young men, and all three are indicative as to how any organisation should work:

- The young men must come first.
- Persistence and perseverance are the two qualities that anyone working with them must have.
- Anyone working with young men selling sex to men must have total dedication and be completely unshakeable.

Conclusion

Working with young men who sell sex to men requires dedication, perseverance, and forward planning, at every level. There must be dedication by the outreach workers, as much of the work can be very difficult, and they need to have a large amount of specialised knowledge to support the needs of young men involved in selling sex. The organisation needs perseverance and must work in the knowledge that no matter how often a young man is referred, he is unlikely to access a service until he is ready to do so. The funders of any project working with young men selling sex must plan a long way in advance, and accept that there is no quick fix for this problem. Only with appropriate funding, equitable support and proper infrastructures will the basic needs of these vulnerable young men be addressed.

CHAPTER 9

BASE: Delivering Services to Young People in Bristol

Di Foley, Joanna Scammel and Rowena Wood

Introduction

Bristol BASE (**B**arnardo's **A**gainst **S**exual **E**xploitation) is a project based in central Bristol to help meet the needs of young people who are involved in, or who are at risk of, commercial sexual exploitation. The project is primarily funded by Barnardo's but receives some funding from Bristol City Council to work with exceptionally vulnerable young people. 'Exceptionally vulnerable' refers to young people who have become isolated from family and peers, who have very few community ties, very low self-esteem and, in most cases, difficulty in making and sustaining relationships. Their vulnerability may derive from factors such as previous sexual, physical or emotional abuse, a lack of boundaries within their families, peer pressures or feeling rejected with no attachments other than with professional bodies.

The service provided through Bristol BASE is still being developed and is rooted in a multi-agency approach to tackling child sexual abuse within Bristol. It is also a central pillar of the Bristol City Council approach to tackling the issue of children who are abused through prostitution or who are at risk of being abused. The Bristol BASE project is the only one in Bristol that is specifically set up to work with children and young people who are being sexually exploited through prostitution. Previously, the work had been focused on girls and young women who have been looked after by the local authority, and worked with them on issues of sexual safety, sexual health and personal relationships. The project is developing and expanding and with that comes a service which can now be accessed by young men, who can self refer or who can be referred by other agencies, making the service more accessible and inclusive for all children and young people.

Bristol BASE has worked tirelessly in raising awareness of the issue of commercial sexual exploitation of young people. This has involved taking into account the wider picture where there are growing concerns about crime related incidents that are linked to the commercial sexual exploitation of children and young people, a growing drug culture, and a high incidence of violence and sexual assaults. We have evidence of this through working with young people who have been targeted by predatory males.

Gender and ethnicity of the young people

When facilitating training and raising awareness within the community, and with other agencies, about the commercial sexual exploitation of children and young people, BASE has always included the issue of young men who are involved in prostitution. This appears to be a more difficult area of work for other agencies to recognise and respond to, however, and is reflected in the small numbers of young men we have worked with (13 young men 2001–2002).

Staff at BASE have also monitored the ethnicity of young people who are at risk or who are involved in commercial sexual exploitation. The majority of young people we work with are white UK but we would question whether young people from black and ethnic minority groups who are at risk of being sexually exploited are slipping through the net. This is because workers in many agencies appear to feel unable to address the needs of this group, because of the sensitive nature of the work, and the diverse cultural backgrounds from which the young people come. We also feel that the commercial sexual exploitation of young people from minority ethnic communities is more likely to be hidden i.e. in private flats or massage parlours. We believe this may be the case because these young people tend to come from small, close communities therefore making the young people who may be involved more identifiable within the community.

Referrals

The majority of children/young people who receive a service (80 per cent) are referred by Bristol Social Services. Through proactive awareness raising of the issues for young people involved in commercial sexual exploitation, and networking with a variety of other agencies in both voluntary and statutory sectors, we now have an open referral system in place. This involves agencies contacting us either to make initial enquires about the service or with information or concerns about a young person. We would then send information or explain the service that is available and await a response from the referrer, as we would not work with any young person without their consent. If the young person agrees to receive a service, the referrer would then make arrangements for the young person to meet with a worker from BASE. The service is available to all young people between the ages of ten and 18 years of age (21 years of age if the young person has been looked after by the local authority). This includes young people who may self-refer or request a service.

More recently we have secured the services of Connexions who provide an on-site surgery once a week and a young persons' drug worker. We also provide a sexual health /contraceptive service for young people but this part is funded through a Home Office funded initiative, the Pandora project. This is discussed more fully below.

Good experiences for all children

The project strives to make this a priority, with work concentrating on continual consultation with children and young people, listening to their needs, being positive and realistic about their visions and allowing them to be children. Underpinning the work that we do with young people who are at risk of, or involved in commercial sexual exploitation, is the relationship between the worker and the young person. 80 per cent of the young people that we work with have historical sexual abuse issues and reports from agencies working with young people who survive sexual abuse often highlight the significance of at least one supportive relationship in helping young people to survive.

As a team we talk about 'getting alongside' young people, and have a shared understanding of what this means. It can refer to how we relate initially to the young people who are referred to the project. This aspect is vital in that it lays the groundwork in forming a relationship based on trust and mutual understanding. In achieving this, it is important to find out what the young person is interested in; it may be music, DJs, friendships, family, personal relationships, TV soaps, sports, clothes and so on. It can take time to begin to discuss some of the problems that the young person is experiencing, and it is important to give them this time. TV soaps can play a role in discussing issues in a safe way, so that initially personal disclosures are not involved.

Team members share their experiences and support each other through what can be very challenging and, at times, difficult and disturbing situations. All our work rests on social work values of acceptance and respect as recommended by the Central Council for Education and Training in Social Work (CCETSW). These values are vital in enabling young people to accept themselves, and develop a sense of self-esteem. Self-acceptance and self-esteem are the essential perquisites to making positive changes.

Many of the young people who come to BASE have experienced parental separation, they have been 'Looked After' by the local authority, and have moved from children's homes or foster carers on a number of occasions. Such experiences can result in damaging attachment behaviour, which can lead to problems with the development of a sense of self, and self-esteem. As a result of this, young people can find it difficult to seek the support that they need or to trust anyone who is offering support. Their expectation is often rejection and their behaviour can be extremely challenging when testing this. The skills we use when listening to young people and gaining an understanding of what is going on for them stem from counselling.

Having a genuine concern for the person is the foundation from which we develop a working relationship and we engage young people in all aspects of the decision making process. This in turn can enable young people to express their ideas and have them validated. This is crucial to building a relationship based on trust, which in turn can enhance a young person's sense of self-worth. Within this we are also quite clear with the young person that BASE is a child care agency and, as such, we have a duty to abide by child protection procedures.

Service delivery is important to all those who work at the project, including clerical staff who are often the first person the young people meet when they enter the building. Many of the young people who come to the project will have experienced negative and discriminatory attitudes, some of which they may have internalised. Valuing young people and the implementation of effective anti-discriminatory practice is crucial to our work. If we fail to recognise their cultural differences, or ignore experiences of racism, sexism, or exploitation, then we fail to understand the young person's social reality.

BASE offers a safe environment where young people are able to express themselves without feeling judged. It is an environment in which they are listened to and where boundaries of confidentiality are clearly understood. The physical environment, i.e. the building itself, plays a significant part in setting the scene. It is an attractive and comfortable environment where young people are able to relax.

Another essential element of our work is to recognise the strengths and resilience of young people. The stories young people tell us about their lives can be overwhelming, and whilst these feelings need to be recognised and talked through with colleagues, it is important to remember how resilient the young people are. If we focus only on their traumatic experiences, it can suggest that they will be unable to move on and improve the quality of their lives.

Whilst we acknowledge the problems that young people may have experienced, we also try to focus on their achievements and strengths. Through doing so, we are able to offer a service that aims for more than just survival of commercial sexual exploitation.

Inter-agency work

In order that we may bring about change for young people it is important to listen to the young people, assess their needs and have links with other agencies who are best placed to address some of these needs. BASE therefore works closely with the Police Child Protection Team, district police

Table 1: Services provided by Barnardos' BASE

The Project

The Project provides the following services:

- **Individual casework with young people:** We address the issues that the young people feel are pressing (often the referrer will cite what they feel the issues are and these are often different from what the young person considers the issues to be). The worker will review the work with the young person every six weeks and the young person participates fully in this process.

- **Preventive work with young people:** We facilitate training in schools with young people about personal relationships, abusive relationships and the process of entrapment. We examine with young people concerns about abusive relationships, what the concerns are and how to take this forward. We explore with the young person issues of personal and sexual safety, their self-esteem and understanding of the situations in which they find themselves.

- **Support work with other professionals:** This includes attending strategy meetings on young people who are at risk of sexual exploitation and being included in an action plan for the young person. We give information and advice about the service and the criteria for referring young people. BASE facilitates training on sexual exploitation for the Area Child Protection Committee and other agencies, for example, Connexions, social services and education departments.

- **Case planning and advice:** We work jointly with other agencies when a number of issues and concerns presented by the young person may impact on service provision. For example, homelessness may keep a young person in an unsafe environment and render them vulnerable to involvement in commercial sexual exploitation. If the young person has a drug habit, this would then impact on what housing is available and its suitability. Often in this situation, poor quality housing is offered. BASE often acts as advocates for the young person, meeting with other professionals and negotiating with and on the young person's behalf.

- **Drop-in and sessional support for vulnerable young people:** When young people are in crisis or when practical assistance is required, young people visit the project without appointment. In this instance, a worker would always be available to see the young person.

---

and social services. Since 2001 BASE has been involved with other voluntary as well as statutory agencies in the Home Office funded Pandora Project.

The Pandora Project

The Bristol Prostitution Forum consists of agencies, community representatives and city councillors who are concerned about prostitution in certain areas of Bristol and about the impact this activity is having on the community. At one meeting of the forum, the issue of children who are abused through prostitution was raised and it was agreed, in the spirit of *Working Together to Safeguard Children* (DoH, 1999), that a multi-agency project would be best placed to address this issue. The project is named the Pandora Project. The service provides advice and individual assistance to young people on a range of issues, for example, relationships, sexual health, self-esteem, drugs and sexuality. The Pandora Project is funded by the Home Office Crime Reduction Programme and supported by Bristol City Council, the Police Child Protection Team, social services, Terence Higgins Trust, Barnardo's BASE, Bristol Drugs Project, 125, and Bristol Community Safety.

The work of Bristol BASE is normally project based, but being involved with the Pandora Project gave us the opportunity, through outreach work, to explore the street scene in relation to juvenile prostitution in Bristol with a partner drugs agency. This consisted of two half time outreach workers.

Outreach

The outreach workers in Bristol cover a large area of the inner city where street prostitution exists. These 'red light' areas are spreading and have become almost impossible to work on foot. There is evidence that the areas traditionally used are changing and young people have been seen working outside of these areas. This could be because of the high level of policing in the known areas. Bristol BASE has a personal safety policy, and has issued the workers with white jackets making them identifiable to the police and the young women. They also inform the police when they are going to do outreach.

The Bristol BASE workers have a driver who drops them off in the areas in which prostitution takes place. The driver's role involves observation and ensuring that the outreach work on foot is as safe as possible. The driver always keeps the workers in sight and notes car registration numbers of kerb crawlers and men who are believed to be involved in coercing young women into prostitution. This information is passed to the police. The very nature of outreach work called for the workers to engage with young people on the street. This meant that the work was live, dynamic, had a life of its own, and could be dangerous. As a result of the outreach work, we have managed to offer services to very young girls who have needed to see our nurses for sexual health checks. Some young people come into the BASE project for regular advice or support or to access drug services.

The majority of young people with whom the workers come into contact are white UK females. They tend to come from Bristol or surrounding areas. Their ages range from 14 to 21. A large proportion of them come from local authority care or local hostels, they also tend to stay in flats used for drug taking and dealing. The activity of outreach work is becoming increasingly dangerous. In recent years, there has been a noticeable change in the street scene in Bristol mainly due to the rise in crack cocaine users on the streets. This has led to young people taking greater risks. Some of these risks have involved very young people being used as 'runners' for the drug dealers. We see this as their initiation into drug use as well as an introduction into commercial sexual exploitation. There have also been reports from the public that young women have been seen on the street as early as 7.30 a.m. The outreach workers have covered these times but have as yet been unable to make contact with anyone.

Most of the young girls contacted through outreach are drug dependent. There are reports from the girls that they 'binge out' on crack cocaine for days on end in an ever-increasing number of crack houses. These are places in which the commercial sexual exploitation of children and young people can flourish as the girls that use the drug are often given small amounts in return for sex. These venues may provide shelter and accommodation for those children who have run away from home or local authority care or for whom a foster placement has broken down. They are dangerous and extremely hard to reach environments in which reports of rapes and sexual assaults are not uncommon. Health risks appear to be greater for the young women who go to the crack houses and there is growing evidence from them that the men they become involved with in these places are men who do not use condoms. In summary, our experience in outreach work indicates that:

- The change in drugs being used from heroin, now often in conjunction with crack cocaine, has led to the young women taking greater risks.
- There appear to be more young women on the street.
- The street work has become more dangerous for the young women, and there are more sexual and physical attacks upon them.

Health provision

In relation to the Pandora Project, BASE hosts the sexual health input on site. Many of the young women with whom we work, or with whom the outreach workers have made contact, are given the opportunity to have their health needs addressed by two sexual health nurses who are experienced in working with this client group. The health needs of these young people are much wider than sexual health and we have worked with and helped young women to access primary health care, i.e. general practitioners. This has sometimes been difficult, especially if the young person is drug dependent, because this has an impact on whether a GP is prepared to register a young person.

The lifestyle led by young people on the streets takes its toll on their health, through bad diet, lack of care, use of a combination of drugs and so on. Often this presents itself in other forms, for example, young women have been seen with extreme skin complaints, weeping ulcers that are untreated and infected impetigo. The physical and mental health issues that some of the young people present have often been ignored by the young people themselves and by professionals with whom they may have been in contact who may not connect self-harming, eating disorders, and so forth, with abuse. BASE does address some of these issues with the young people in the hope that they will access the appropriate services that can help them to recover.

Housing

In raising the issue of housing, it should be recorded that the outreach workers have to date only ever met one girl who is still living at home with her mother. Housing is an enormous issue for the young people that we come into contact with. Recently, a 15-year-old who is involved in commercial sexual exploitation told the workers that a large proportion of the money she earns is spent on hotel rooms. She feels that this is a more attractive option for her than to go back to her foster placement, which has recently broken down.

Basic and popular psychology such as that proposed by Maslow has long suggested that until human beings have certain basic needs met they will be unable to move on to further development and life stages. When this theory is applied to this particular group, it becomes clear that until we have resources such as adequate housing at our disposal, the job of promoting recovery and healing from the effects of commercial sexual exploitation is likely to continue to be difficult.

Child protection

BASE works closely with the child protection team, which was influential in placing commercial sexual exploitation of children on the agenda within Avon and Somerset Constabulary. The Pandora Project has brought together agencies that are signed up to the policies developed by the Area Child

Protection Committee. These different agencies have the necessary skills and experience of working with children and young people on issues that may contribute to their sexual abuse through prostitution, for example, drugs, separation, loss, rejection, neglect or abuse.

The Child Protection Team Officers, who have been designated to work with this client group, have demonstrated that it is possible for statutory and voluntary agencies to work together, building a trust that is visible for the young people to see. The knock-on effect of this is that children and young people are now more likely to assist the police or exchange information about the street scene, dangerous men and so on. This is evident in current practice.

The Bristol Department of Social Services has also played a vital role in exchanging information and identifying young women who have been reported as missing. Positive action, which included discussions with local authorities who have a responsibility to the young women identified, has resulted in appropriate services being put in place. The social services department has been proactive about Pandora, and is raising awareness amongst social work practitioners. This includes having designated officers who link with the partner agencies of Pandora in line with the Department of Health/Home Office Guidance (DoH/HO/DfEE, 2000).

Bristol Social Services has been instrumental in facilitating multi-agency practice forums. They have, for example, co-ordinated a task group of all child care agencies to address some of the relevant issues. This has enabled agencies to explore positive action and options for young people who may be involved in commercial sexual exploitation. Working in partnership, with statutory as well as voluntary agencies, has led to training days for multi-agency staff teams. The local authority also has a policy and protocol in place, as per '*Safeguarding Children Involved in Prostitution*' (DoH/HO/DfEE, 2000) which is prescriptive and clear about procedures when dealing with children involved in commercial sexual exploitation. BASE has a close working relationship with the authority.

The team is continually developing and learning. This has been facilitated by the ability to discuss openly within the team, and the organisation, practice issues. This enables practitioners to contribute and share their knowledge of this work, which is still relatively new. Developing this service, however, and responding to the needs of these young people, has not been plain sailing. There have been obstacles to surmount, some of which are listed below.

Issues in outreach and street work

- Obtaining the young women's real names and ages has proved a difficult task. This is no doubt due to a number of factors – the young women may have little or no trust left in adults, they have also probably been threatened by whomever is working them and warned that they are never to give out their real details to anyone. This makes it extremely difficult to pass precise details onto the Police Child Protection Teams and other statutory agencies.

- Contacting the police on the telephone has often proved an arduous task. It takes a considerable amount of time to get through to the police, explain your position and await a response. This process has presented the workers with a real dilemma especially when they have within their sight a young person who they know will vanish from sight within minutes.

- The population of young girls out on the streets is dynamic and constantly changing. We have heard it said that these young people have 'floating lives'. This would seem to be true as we often meet young girls who have come into Bristol from surrounding areas and cities. They may stay for a short while and then vanish again, indeed it is not uncommon for us to establish rapport with a young person and then not see them for weeks. It seems a lot of their actions and whereabouts will depend on the orders given to them by the abusive adult who is exploiting them.

- Bristol has a growing number of Jamaican nationals, many of whom are thought to be in the country illegally and who are allegedly involved in criminal activity. A number of the young girls we meet on outreach have been targeted, and are now being worked, by these men. The girls are constantly describing them as 'violent' and 'dangerous'. Sexual assaults and rape are becoming commonplace and occur on a regular basis. Sadly, for reasons of our own safety, we have had to avoid some of the more prominent areas that are used by some of the young people. It is not uncommon, for example, for the outreach workers to be approached by a car full of these men, and this experience is extremely intimidating.

Practice issues

- There is a need for us to re-visit our aims and to examine the positive and negative aspects of our learning from working together. In addition, we need to explore how to take the work forward. This is a particular concern in relation to outreach work because the funding for this element of practice is precarious.

- Building relationships with young people who are in controlling and/or abusive relationships is often difficult due to their mistrust of adults.

- Outreach work is certainly changing as a result of an increase in drug use and a feeling of high energy on the streets. Although we are contacting increasing numbers of young people, relatively few are accessing services

- New legislation that gives the police greater powers in relation to kerb crawlers has resulted in a heavy police presence on the streets. The implication of this is that young people may use off street sites, which we would not be able to access, hence making contact with young people extremely hard.
- Although information between the agencies about young people seen on the street is shared, the fact that no referral system is in place within the Pandora partnership can create confusion about who is working with whom.

BASE is a very small team of dedicated senior social work practitioners, who have all contributed to this chapter. In view of our very limited resources, we are proud of what we do and what we have achieved. We know that we have made a difference in the lives of some of the young people that we have worked with because they have told us so.

Conclusions

BASE works with 'hard to reach' young people, who nevertheless do attend appointments with the workers. This in itself is an indication that they are in need of support, as the services offered through BASE and Pandora is a voluntary service. The young people's involvement with both BASE and Pandora through outreach has given the workers an insight into the chaotic and dangerous lifestyles of women and children who are involved in commercial sexual exploitation in Bristol. We are sure that the young women are not choosing to live this life. The vulnerability of, and extreme risks taken by, this group are clearly visible. These are often presented through physical or sexual violence, and give an insight into the hopelessness that the young people often express and experience.

This feeling of hopelessness is often talked about by the workers who themselves feel that they are only scratching the surface in terms of the work that they could do if resources were available. They are frustrated by the lack of housing, detox facilities and often, practical support – for example, having access to showers and clean clothes. These have often not been available at the times when they are most needed. This can be addressed through the continuation of this project with extended opening times of BASE who would provide practical support as well as providing a face to face service.

In terms of the multi-agency partnership, learning from each other and exploring ways forward, has on the whole been a positive experience. The Pandora Project, however, is still in the development stage and needs ongoing resources to enable the excellent work it has undertaken to continue. An analysis of the strengths, needs, opportunities and threats experienced by the BASE project is provided below:

Bristol BASE

Strengths

- New premises.
- Strong local networks and effective inter-agency working.
- Good internal relationships e.g. trust.
- Strong reputation of BASE team within Bristol.
- Strong practice base in specialist area.
- Opportunity to develop a more holistic service including:

Specialist drug/alcohol/mental health worker input.
Preventative strategies.
External consultancy work.
Training development functions.

Needs

- Thin external funding opportunities.
- Growing recognition of BASE work but inadequate resources to respond.
- Therapeutic support to families.
- Lack of resources to develop preventative services i.e. education.
- Lack of health funding.
- Input into emotional/mental health needs of young people who are being sexually exploited.
- Move on accommodation.

Opportunities

- Implementation of government/HO guidelines on strategy meetings for young people.
- Develop work with young men, building on existing pilot work.
- Development of specialist funding opportunities such as housing or economic regeneration.
- New joint working initiatives following Pandora.
- New health priorities.

Threats

- Lack of financial resources.
- Adult services working with young people outside of child protection protocols.

CHAPTER 10

The Genesis Project: Meeting the Needs of Young Women in Leeds

Lisa Wilkinson-Shaw

Introduction

The Genesis project is a voluntary sector service in Leeds that aims to meet the needs of women who are involved in, or at risk of involvement in, prostitution. The organisation was established ten years ago and developed as a result of members of a local church organisation realising that there was no agency working in Leeds to meet the needs of this client group. A member of the church organisation volunteered to work with the women and initially attempted to make contact with them on the street. Because she was unknown to them, the women concerned were suspicious of her and she failed to establish contact. She was even reported to the police by the women themselves. In an attempt to engage the women, the volunteer began to attend the local magistrate's court regularly when the women were appearing for soliciting offences. She would chat to them briefly about their lives and offered to advocate for them in court to which the women agreed. She would relay to the magistrates the sorts of lives the women were leading and explain the difficulties associated with paying fines. As a result, many of the fines were reduced or quashed.

The project has grown steadily and successfully since it was first established and now has two and a half paid posts to work with adult women and one paid worker to work with under 18-year-olds – a post that was created two years ago. The project still relies heavily on volunteers – currently there are four who have been trained and 14 who are in the process of induction. The induction lasts ten weeks and is quite vigorous and intense. Some of the volunteers don't make it through this period but those who do, come from a variety of backgrounds. Currently, for example, there is a trainee doctor and a DJ amongst the volunteers. All the volunteers make a valuable contribution to the service.

The project provides advice, advocacy and support for adult women and young women (under 18) at risk or involved in prostitution through drop-in, one-to-one work and outreach services. This chapter describes some of the work we do, how we do it and the difficulties and challenges we face in that work.

Confidentiality

The project operates what might be described as a 'high-risk' confidentiality policy. This means that we allow the women themselves (whether they are over or under 18) to determine what information we share about them and with whom we share it. This is about letting the women themselves have some control over what information they wish us to share with other agencies. Our experience is that many of the women have experienced a variety of systems throughout their lives – such as the care system – where files have been held and information shared about their lives and they have never felt they had control over that. We believe therefore that our confidentiality policy empowers the young women and it is one of the reasons they keep coming back to the project. They tell us things about their lives because they know we are not going to divulge them to anyone else. In the case of a young person under 18, the circumstances in which confidentiality will be breached are made clear to them from the outset. These are when a young person discloses information that suggests she is putting herself more at risk than she does every night by being on the street. In circumstances other than these, we do not share information about the young woman with other agencies unless we have her express permission to do so.

Although this may sound alien to practitioners in other agencies, files are not kept on individual women and case notes are not recorded. Our confidentiality policy does at times appear to alarm other agencies such as social services and they tend to see what we *don't* do rather than what we *can* do. However, we also work with social services as they have a statutory responsibility towards the young women, especially if they are accommodated or looked after by the local authority. We have on a number of occasions successfully facilitated the re-establishment of relationships between young women and their social workers. This would happen on a 'negative consent' basis. If social services were to contact us to ask if we were in touch with a particular young woman, our response would be, 'We are not able to divulge that but we will look out for her and tell her that you want to get in touch or that you are worried'.

We carry this 'high-risk' policy because we feel that if we were to breach the young woman's confidentiality we might lose contact with her altogether. This would be unhelpful, as we may be the only agency with whom she has any contact. Maintaining confidentiality however does not involve colluding with the young woman's behaviour – she would be encouraged to contact her social worker or to allow a project worker to do that on her behalf. In situations such as these, we would tell the young woman that her social worker has phoned us and that she wants to get in touch with her. We would then ask the young woman what she wants to do. Usually in these circumstances, we have managed to get the young woman to consent to meet with or speak to the social worker but she may request that we do not tell the social worker where she is living. We would grant her request in these circumstances and not disclose her address. If the young woman were to say that she did not want any contact with the social worker and did not want us to make contact on her behalf, a risk assessment would be undertaken and, depending on the results of that, confidentiality would be breached or not. In most cases, it has not been and we have found this has worked very well in the ten years we have been established.

Through such practices, we believe it is possible to maintain confidentiality but at the same time keep the young woman as safe as possible in an empowering way.

Scale of the problem

We do not know how many young people are at risk of or are involved in commercial sexual exploitation in Leeds. Currently we work with approximately 20 young women on an individual basis. They are all involved in street prostitution rather than working from flats or saunas. Some have told us that they first became involved in prostitution when they were just 10-years-old (not usually working from the street) and that they have been using heroin since they were 12. Most have drug dependencies (90 per cent of all those we work with) and are using drugs such as heroin or crack-cocaine. Crack appears to be their drug of 'choice' and the more they earn the more of it they use. Currently, only one of the under 18s we work with is not using crack or heroin although she does use alcohol and her vulnerability suggests that she will probably start using heroin in time. We are now frequently and increasingly seeing young women who are 'working' to support their drug habits and usually their partners' as well. These young women tend to lead extremely chaotic lifestyles; some have mental health problems and some are heavily pimped. When they are engaged with pimps they tend to be very guarded and it is often difficult for project workers to engage them.

The area in which street prostitution takes place in Leeds has become more dispersed over the past two or three years and is now spread across two police divisions. There has been a police campaign to remove prostitution from the known 'red light' areas and as a result the area where street prostitution occurs has become more geographically scattered and less concentrated in one or two areas.

Outreach work

Outreach forms the core of our work with this client group although it is not specifically aimed at young people. It is always undertaken in pairs and usually with the aid of volunteers. Outreach takes place on Tuesdays and Wednesdays from eight o'clock onwards. On one night, we undertake joint work with a local drug project and on another with a hepatitis B nurse. The Genesis project has just acquired a van that is completely fitted out for outreach work. In the first section, there are benches with enough room for six people to sit, there is also a little kitchenette and a space for the nurse to see the women. We provide coffees and distribute condoms and so forth. We go to the areas in which the women are working and they come to the van. They get to know about us through word of mouth. Some come in just to get warm and have a coffee. The outreach is the only contact we have with some women, as they will not come into the premises in which Genesis is housed for drop-in sessions. In summary, the core services provided by outreach are:

- Harm reduction/minimisation around sex work and drug use (needle exchange, condoms, health checks).
- Hepatitis B vaccinations.
- Somewhere for the women to come and chat, have a coffee and a point of contact with the service.

On/off street locations

We do get some young people working in saunas but there are not that many that we are aware of. This is primarily because these premises are at risk of being raided by the police and many sauna owners therefore do not want them in there if they are underage. We think there may be some very young people working from flats. Those who have told us they began working when they were ten said they were working from houses, flats or their homes depending on who had introduced them to prostitution. Pimps would be unlikely to work very young girls from the streets as they would face serious risks of being caught – older working women would be likely to report them, for example. The older women hate to see young girls on the street. We believe this is either because they remind them of themselves or because they understand how harsh and violent the world of prostitution is. The very young girls who are involved are well hidden and we have great difficulty in accessing them.

Some women would not in any case work in saunas even if the owners allowed them to. However, there are those who frequently go from saunas to the street but there are also those who work in saunas who have never done street work and would never dream of doing it. Some women have chosen to go into saunas because they prefer it to street work but for many that choice is becoming more limited because of their drug use. Lots of saunas will not take women who are using drugs. That means many do not admit to using drugs when they start but then they get found out and get sacked. Also, a lot of drug users could not possibly sustain the 12-hour shifts that are expected of them in saunas.

Some women appear to prefer work in off-street locations because they believe it to be safer than on street. However, wherever they choose to work, there is always an element of risk involved.

Whole people

The Genesis project treats the women we work with as 'whole' people and we approach them holistically. We do not just work with them about their lives on the streets but also around other aspects of their lives and experiences. In addition to attempting to empower the young women and allow them to gain control through allowing them to decide what information is shared about them and with whom, we go to court with them and advocate for them in legal matters. We also accompany them to housing departments to help them address their housing problems and attend case conferences with them. Many of the women we work with have had their children removed from them – some of them because they were involved in prostitution and others because they were involved in drug use and not being responsible parents.

We also run a 'dodgy punters' scheme and complete violent incident reports. When the women tell us they have been involved in a violent incident with a punter or pimp, this is recorded in a book so that other women know to look out for them. We also fill in incident reports for the police. These are done anonymously on a two-sided sheet of paper. This provides a detailed description of the man or men involved, whether they were driving a car or whether they were in taxis. A brief outline of the incident is also provided and, at the bottom of the sheet, we say whether the woman concerned wishes to remain anonymous or whether she is prepared to make a statement. That is then passed on to intelligence officers. We do not operate any confidentiality policy in relation to punters or pimps so we would always relay that sort of information back to the police and that works quite well.

To summarise, some of the key activities in terms of supporting these young women, in addition to those provided through outreach, involve:

- Advocating for them at court.
- Helping with money management or coping with debts.
- Supporting them at case conferences.
- Supporting them if their children are removed from them.
- Providing assistance with housing problems (accompanying them to the housing department and so on).
- Recording and reporting violent incidents.
- Supporting them through the emotional trauma of violence from partners, punters or pimps.

- Advocating for them to receive appropriate services and interventions from statutory agencies, for example drug detoxification facilities.

How we do what we do

The principles that govern our work at Genesis are to advocate for and support those who are at risk or involved in prostitution. Our aims are not primarily to stop them working or to 'rescue' them. We tend to avoid the term 'victim' as we consider it to be hugely disempowering. Obviously, we do not encourage young women to stay in prostitution because it is proven to be a very damaging lifestyle. What we try to establish is a trusting relationship with the young woman. Her experiences with the worker and what may constitute her first trusting relationship might then be the way forward to looking at exiting from the lifestyle in which she is involved. For those who may have been involved in prostitution for a while, that can be a very long process but for those who are new to the street, we would try to get them out of it as soon as we could.

For those who have been involved in the 'street scene' for a while, we consider that prostitution and drug use become a lifestyle. Exiting prostitution is therefore not like packing in a job at Tescos and the idea that one can just leave prostitution and go to stack shelves at Sainsbury's is fanciful to say the least. We know from our experience in this work that it does not happen that way and consider that it would be naïve, offensive and insulting of us to say to a young woman, 'Come on, we've got to get you out of it'. If, on the other hand, a young woman were to say to us, 'I hate it, I've got to stop', then we would say, 'Right, let's do it'.

We acknowledge that prostitution is a choice, a very limited choice but a choice nevertheless. Who is to say for a 17-year-old that it is not a choice? Although we believe that it is abusive and damaging, we also recognise that for that particular young woman, it may be the only thing that appears to be a possibility for her at that time and it is perhaps the safest thing she knows. She hates being beaten regularly and being pimped, but at the same time, she knows what is coming and what to expect. It is predictable and that is safe for her. She may even still say, 'I love him. Nobody has ever loved me like he has. What's the alternative? To be in care with 15 other young people being looked after because people are paid to look after me, not being loved?'

In realistic terms, the workers at this project are unable to offer anything in the way of a viable alternative and it would be unrealistic and unfair to pretend that we can. We are not going to take her home with us after all! We do try, however, to offer appropriate interventions and support. If it is drugs, for example, that have brought her to the street, which seems to be happening with increasing frequency now, we try to let them know of initiatives that are going on in relation to that. We put them in touch with agencies that can deal with their drug issues and there is a rehabilitation clinic that we can try to get them into. We have to try to get them plugged into drug treatment services before their drug use has become entrenched and before the behaviour patterns have become so well rehearsed that the patterns of behaviour are almost impossible to break. In this sense, we tend to relate the situations of many of the young girls involved in prostitution to situations of domestic violence. Women who become stuck in those situations also tend to find it hard to leave. It may be easier to leave a situation of domestic violence after the first instance rather than when the pattern of abuse has become established over time.

When they are already involved in prostitution, we also try to promote safer working practices because it is our view that the problem is not so much that they are working but that they are working in unsafe environments. Our aim is therefore obviously to address that issue and suggest ways through which they may be able to work more safely. That might be in relation to environmental issues, for example, working on the street. In these circumstances, we might ask them whether they have tried or considered working from saunas, flats or home.

Preventative work

Since it was initiated, the project has always worked with young women but it is only in the past two years that a post has been created specifically to focus on this work. Our work with young people is now much more proactive than it previously was. We have established links with schools and residential units and have recently developed joint work with a Child Protection Co-ordinator for Education within the city. This is taking our work into schools and focusing on prevention, because young girls in schools do not believe that they might be groomed and pimped and possibly exploited. We do not go into schools and start talking about prostitution, but instead we talk about exploitation within normal relationships. We discuss how disrespect occurs, how there is a need for them to value themselves within relationships, how they need to be confident about what they want and not allow that to be compromised. We also encourage them to recognise when someone might be abusing them physically or emotionally and to think about where that might lead. Our aim is to get them to believe in themselves and to trust in what they want from a relationship. We believe that equipping them to think in this way gives them strength in relation to decision making so that if they meet anyone who may be likely to exploit them they might recognise certain signs and be able to say, 'No, that isn't what I want'.

The preventative work we undertake is conducted, of course, alongside the ongoing one-to-one work in which we are involved as well as the outreach work.

Accessing services

At the time the Genesis project was established in Leeds, there were no other agencies providing for the needs of this client group – either for adults or children. Our work has demonstrated that many of the women we work with tend not to access other services, for example, health services, GU medicine, drug services and so forth. This is often due to their experiences of discrimination and prejudice or the anticipation that they will encounter such attitudes from mainstream service providers. It is also due to their low self-esteem and their belief that everyone knows that they are working. In terms of medical treatment, for example, a young woman would probably not want to divulge to her GP that she is involved in prostitution. A GP confronted with a young woman asking for a cap might be inclined to enquire why she might need one if she is on the pill or has been sterilised while we, on the other hand, would advocate that women use caps and diaphragms for when they are menstruating.

The young people with whom we work have a range of complex needs – some have mental health or drug problems. Their drug problems, especially if they are using crack, also lead to other health problems. Crack tends to lead them to pick at themselves leaving some of them with big holes in their faces and bodies where they have been scratching. For a while a number of the women had impetigo where they were just covered in sores. There has been a huge increase in the rate of hepatitis C and many of the women we work with are hepatitis C positive. It seems that many of them use condoms when they are working to protect against sexually transmitted diseases but they share needles with other drug users and do not always remember with whom they have shared them. This of course has huge implications for their long-term health. Apart from health issues, the women may need advice in relation to debt or legal issues while some need advice about housing and so on. Many may need support in relation to all of these issues.

We find that in many instances, the attitudes of practitioners in statutory agencies are not conducive to developing effective interventions with this group. For example, practitioners in social services may make judgements about whether or not our clients make good parents while the police make judgements about the young women and tend to regard rape as just a 'hazard of the job'. Additionally, housing officers make judgements about whether these young women should be housed as priority one for fleeing violence and tend to hold the view that they have 'brought it on themselves'

Our ability to meet and respond to these various levels of need is hindered by the fact that we are a small charitable organisation with a full staff team of only six (and this includes an administrator). One of the biggest challenges we face in the work we undertake with these young people is that we simply do not have the resources to respond. We believe that statutory services need to accept a greater share of responsibility for this group although we recognise that they too are struggling with limited resources. This can be illustrated by way of case study example but we have numerous examples of these young women being inadequately provided for by statutory services.

One of our clients, who for these purposes we will refer to as Kerry, regularly self-harms and overdoses. She likes hospital and the attention she receives when she is in there. She is very needy and demanding and crying out for help. When she is in hospital, psychiatric assessments are undertaken to determine whether or not she is going to kill herself. As most of her self-harming and overdosing is attention seeking or crying for help she probably will not. Thus she is discharged again and returned to a residential unit with people not knowing where she is going or what she is doing. Our role in those circumstances is to advocate on the young person's behalf to badger statutory agencies to develop an appropriate care plan for her. What we need desperately is a client-led young people's service – that is, services that are very sympathetic to young people that understand why they might be difficult and why they are reluctant to engage with adults.

Another area of unmet need is for drug treatment services for young people in the city. There is no young person's drug prescribing unit in Leeds, for example, although there is a demonstrable need for one. This may be somewhat controversial, however, as many practitioners do not want to give young people methadone because it is highly addictive. But what is the alternative? One of our clients agreed to go to a rehabilitation unit outside of the area but when social services were approached about this, they were not aware of this facility and did not know where they could access the funds to send her to it. Finally, we accessed the funding for her ourselves and she went to the rehabilitation unit. We managed to get an extension of funding and she was there for 16 weeks. A half way review was supposed to have been conducted but only two workers from our agency turned up for it. What message does that give to the young girl? 'You put me here and I'm doing extremely well, but what package of care have you got for me when I come back? Nothing'.

It is not good enough that there are not enough resources. That young person needed to feel that she was valued and that people cared about her but no care or support plan was prepared for her when she came out. She has therefore, quite understandably, sabotaged the detoxification programme by leaving it. She thinks, 'There is no way you are going to let me down again so I'll do it myself because you expect me to fail anyway'. This particular young woman is now back on heroin and crack. In another example, eight practitioners turned up for the half way review. The young woman knew that when she came out there would be all these people there to support her – this gives a very different message – and a very important one for extremely vulnerable young people.

New government guidance

The government has recommended that young people involved in prostitution should be brought within child protection procedures because they are 'children in need' who are suffering or likely to suffer 'significant harm' (DoH/HO/DfEE, 2000). It is recognised that these are not young people making informed choices yet somehow, because there is money (or drugs) changing hands, their abuse is regarded differently from other young people who experience sexual abuse. If an uncle were abusing his niece or a teacher one of his pupils, there would be uproar. The fact that in some instances punters appear to be asking older working women if there are any pre-pubescent girls (no pubic hair or hips) available, appears not to evoke the same response – either from the public or from those agencies charged with responsibilities for caring for children and young people.

Government guidance recommends that a child under the age of 18 should not be cautioned or charged with offences related to loitering and soliciting. It is our experience, however that this is not happening. When they are under 16 they are not being cautioned and charged but as soon as they reach 16, policemen in our area are continuing to caution and charge them. This is unfortunate, as it indicates that the police are not making a distinction between these young people and adults and therefore not taking account of these young people's lives. We have found that there is variability in police response to this issue depending on the rank of the officer (generally the higher their rank the more aware of the issue and how to deal with it they are) and the particular police unit they work within. We have found for example, that certain divisions within the police do not know of what Genesis does because different divisions appear not to talk to each other. In one area, while one division of the police was aware of the new protocols for dealing with juveniles involved in prostitution, the traffic police were busy arresting and cautioning a 15-year-old girl for loitering and soliciting and locking her in the cells for the night.

It may be that as practitioners in all agencies become more aware of the provisions made by the new guidance things will change in time – for example, there are now numerous community penalties that can be used. This demonstrates a need for agencies such as Genesis to work with statutory agencies in a multi-disciplinary way to develop effective exit strategies for the young people who are involved. Currently there are no such strategies in place and we have nothing whatsoever to offer these young people. ACPC procedures need to place the responsibility for developing such strategies firmly with statutory services and the resources need to be forthcoming in order to develop and implement them. Otherwise, statutory services will continue to come to organisations such as Genesis to ask what we can do about the problem. If there are robust protocols and procedures in place then statutory agencies are made accountable for the action they must take in relation to this problem. With firm procedures to follow, if it were found that a young person was never in school, a question can be raised about whether she was referred to the exclusion unit. If she was, where did she go from there? If she has been missing, questions can be raised to the police about what they have done to try to find her.

If the guidelines and child protection procedures were to work as they should, when concerns are raised, they can be taken to the ACPC and effective means of dealing with those concerns to prevent the situation from getting any worse can be devised. This is what we are looking at currently within this organisation but it is a massive task and Genesis cannot be the main agency in organising that – it must be the responsibility of statutory social services. We often feel in our organisation that we are being asked to assume the role and responsibility of statutory agencies. We are willing to act as a catalyst and to place the issue firmly on other agencies' agendas but then we feel we should be able to take a back seat and play a supporting rather than a leading role.

Conclusions

This chapter has described the background to the development of the Genesis project and the work it undertakes with young women to support them if they are involved in prostitution or to prevent them from becoming involved if they are considered to be at risk. It demonstrated that the project operates a high-risk confidentiality policy but has shown nevertheless that this is effective in engaging the young women and ensuring that they stay in contact with agency workers.

The chapter has shown that outreach services are an effective method for reaching these young women and that the primary role of this organisation is to advocate on their behalf. The young women are approached holistically and we recognise that, in particular circumstances, prostitution is a choice albeit not one that we would advocate. We also recognise that moving young people away from prostitution is a long process and agencies must be prepared to support them until they decide to exit. Even if they decide to remain in prostitution, they are still in need of support and help and agencies need to be prepared to provide this.

The chapter has also shown that in Leeds, many of the young women have substance misuse problems as well as health and other social problems. They can be difficult to engage and when they are engaged they have a range of complex needs to be met. We have shown in this chapter that in terms of meeting those needs, the biggest challenge is a lack of resources (both for our agency and statutory agencies). We have identified in particular a need for drug treatment services for young people. Additionally, a lack of formalised procedures for dealing with young people who are at risk or involved in prostitution means that statutory agencies tend to neglect their statutory obligations to these young people. We have suggested that, although relationships between statutory and voluntary sector agencies are not always easy, we have some very positive experiences of working with individual social workers and police officers. However, we have indicated in this chapter that if things are going to improve for these young people in this part of the country, formalised procedures to respond to them need to be agreed, adopted and implemented as a matter of some urgency.

CHAPTER 11

Conclusions

Margaret Melrose and David Barrett

Where have we been?

Until relatively recently, the problem of young people sexually exploited through prostitution was consistently denied (see for example Lee and O'Brien, 1995; Barrett, 1997; Brown and Barrett, 2002). It was not a problem that statutory agencies and policy makers were willing to confront. When the problem was acknowledged, it was thought that it was one that involved just a few 'bad girls' in isolated areas of the country – London, Birmingham and perhaps Manchester, for example. It was thought that the way to tackle the problem was to punish these 'bad girls' while letting the men who were paying for their 'services', or profiting obscenely from their involvement in prostitution, off scot-free. Happily, the twenty-first century has witnessed a number of developments in the way these issues are now thought about as the contributors to this volume have demonstrated.

Where are we now?

Although we may still be some way from having a fully comprehensive understanding of the national scale of the problem of young people sexually exploited through prostitution, the work presented in this book begins to provide an indication of its extent across different areas of the country. Most contributors have been surprised at the numbers of young people who are involved in their areas, as they are far greater than they had expected or imagined. These contributions from Bristol, London, Leeds, Nottingham, Sheffield and Wolverhampton dispel the myth that this is a problem confined to major metropolitan or urban areas. We are also clear now that young men, as well as young women, are abused through prostitution and have seen from the contributions in this book that there has been some progress made, in some places, in terms of meeting the needs of young men. It is clear, however, that this area of provision remains relatively underdeveloped and there is still much more that needs to be done. Nevertheless, our understandings of whom, and how many, young people are involved, however, have developed apace in the past five years (Barrett, 1997).

The contributors to this book all demonstrate that they have established effective inter-agency relationships in order to respond to the problem of young people who are sexually exploited through their involvement in prostitution. They demonstrate models of 'joined-up' working that have real and positive effects in the lives of the young people concerned. They also remind us however, that there are no quick answers in this area of work and that the young people may need to be supported over a significant period of time in order to effect change.

Partnership working appears to have been a genuinely positive experience for practitioners. It is heartening to see that in all areas of the country from which the contributions have been drawn, problems in partnership working appear to have been minimised and practitioners have positively embraced new government guidance. This is demonstrated in the different policies and procedures that have been developed to ensure the effective implementation of the new guidelines (DoH/HO/DfEE, 2000). Of course, cynics might say that where partnership working has not been successfully established, and/or where guidelines have not been implemented effectively, practitioners and their senior managers might not have exposed themselves by contributing to a book such as this. In other words, it may be that only those areas with a 'good news' story to tell that agreed to contribute to this book. Some areas that were invited to contribute declined to do so but we know from previous research that the issue of young people exploited through prostitution is equally a problem for local authorities, communities and families in those areas (Melrose et al., 1999). We can be sure, however, that at least in the areas of the country from which these contributions have come, these young people are being responded to as 'children in need', their welfare is being promoted and they are being supported out of prostitution. This represents a huge stride forward given that the guidance is relatively new. There is still more to do, however, to ensure that these models are adopted and developed throughout the country thereby providing children with the protection and support they need and deserve. 'Joined-up' (partnership) working is no longer a choice, from the data presented in this book, it appears to be imperative.

In spite of the good news stories we have presented here, it is important to recognise that the new guidance does, under certain conditions, allow for these young people to be processed through the juvenile justice system in the way that other young offenders are (DoH/HO/DfEE, 2000). These conditions are when young people are considered by those involved in their care to be 'persistently and voluntarily returning to prostitution' (DoH/HO/DfEE, 2000). The meaning of 'persistence' is obviously open to local interpretation and in the future may possibly provide the fuel to fan the flames of conflict between practitioners from different agencies and lead to national variability in the way these young people are responded to. Where and when such conflicts might arise it will be necessary, forcefully, to demonstrate that those who 'persistently' return to prostitution are those who are most vulnerable and most in need of care and protection (Melrose and Barrett,

1999; Melrose and Ayre, 2002). The 'persistence' of such young people will require redoubled persistence on the part of practitioners if they are effectively to engage and work with them. Regardless of how frustrating this work may be at times, it is important to bear in mind that punishment and criminalisation is not an adequate alternative to care and protection.

We understand now that there are multiple factors that lead young people to become involved in prostitution – these range through poverty, homelessness, drug abuse or coercion by abusive adults – and that the young people who become involved experience a number of complex and inter-related problems (Melrose et al., 1999). These include poverty, previous abuse and/or neglect, low self-esteem, low educational attainment and a lack of attachment to supportive social networks. We now appreciate that their needs are *so* complex that *only* a multi-agency approach, with 'joined-up' and seamless services, will provide an adequate and appropriate response (Melrose, 2001). Additionally, we are beginning to comprehend something of the complexity of the routes by which they become involved and are now aware that there is more than one road that leads to the cul-de-sac of prostitution. We know from the contributions in this book, that going missing from home or care places young people at significant risk of becoming involved in commercial sexual exploitation as does involvement in drug use. We have also begun to appreciate that the young people are not necessarily easy to work with or engage and may reject offers of support even when they are most in need of them.

Where are we going?

We see from the evidence presented in these chapters that all practitioners are working in extremely challenging social and economic contexts and that innovative and creative responses, like the examples demonstrated in this book, are needed in order to meet new threats. The young people face enormous risks in terms of their sexual, physical, emotional and psychological health and when they are involved in, or at risk of involvement in, commercial sexual exploitation, they are also vulnerable to other forms of violation and exploitation. They may, for example, be vulnerable to defilement through pornography, rape and sexual assault or through developing drug dependencies.

We have also seen from the contributions in this volume that this work needs to be two-pronged if it is to be effective. At the same time as efforts are made to work with and support the young people, equally vigorous efforts need to be made to develop effective mechanisms to identify and target the men who exploit and abuse them. This is true of men who may pay for their 'services' or who may force them to 'work' in prostitution. Disposing of these men effectively and appropriately will require the co-operation of all criminal justice agencies – the police, the CPS and the courts. When they are prosecuted successfully, the sentences they receive should reflect the severity of the crimes in which they have been involved.

The contributions in this volume suggest that there is a need to work tirelessly to raise awareness of this issue amongst a variety of professional groups. These include amongst others, social work practitioners, health professionals, educationalists and teachers, police officers, teachers, parents and carers, youth workers, elected members and local and national policy makers.

In many areas of the country, despite the excellent work that we have seen is taking place, indications are that generally, as a result of national and international trends (Melrose and Brown, 2002), things look set to get worse in the immediate future – for both the young people and the practitioners trying to work with them. This is particularly as a result of the increased availability of class 'A' drugs such as heroin, cocaine and crack, the increased violence and desperation that accompany their use and the younger ages at which people are beginning to use them (see for example Melrose, 2000a).

The increased availability of drugs on the streets of Britain is not unconnected to the process of globalisation. These forces 'affect and direct all structures and institutions of our present reality and nothing can be understood outside of this context' (Sangera, 1997). These socio-economic processes have resulted in whole communities becoming detached from the economic mainstream and individuals are left to adapt to the new situation through their own devices (Pitts, 2001). These conditions tend to destabilise families, communities and neighbourhoods. As these essential support structures are dislocated, young people are placed in increasingly risky contexts and 'alternative economic opportunities' flourish (Craine, 1997). As young people have been expelled from the labour market and 'placed in a situation of dependence on dwindling welfare benefits', prostitution has become a decreasingly unattractive option for them (Matthews, 1986 cited in Pitts, 1997). The extended process of individualisation that characterises the period in which we live features 'a kind of do-it-yourself biography' which militates against 'stable, monogamous, loving relationships' that were commonplace in previous decades (Scambler and Scambler, 1997: xvii).

In these new conditions, bodies have become increasingly commodified and the bodies of young people have become extremely lucrative commodities in the global market place (Melrose and Brown, 2002). 'Profits from the traffic in human beings amount to $7 billion annually' (UN, 1998b cited in Kelly and Regan, 2000) and it is estimated that 500,000 women were trafficked into the EU in 1995 (IOM, 1996 cited in Kelly and Regan, 2000: 16).

The increase in global traffic in human beings promises only to increase the problems associated with young people who are sexually exploited through prostitution in the UK (Melrose and Brown, 2002).

It is important that in these circumstances, practitioners do not become disheartened. When the going gets (even) tough(er) than it already is, it is important for practitioners to remember the very real difference they make to the lives of these young people and the value the young people place on having someone who is 'there for them'. There will of course be hiccups and some may 'slip off the rails', but if it is possible to engage just one in twenty to support them out of prostitution, then the work has been worthwhile. It is worth reiterating here that this is extremely difficult, and often unrewarding work, especially for those involved at the coalface. It is therefore worth considering the sorts of support mechanisms that might usefully be provided for practitioners to enable them to fulfil most effectively the roles required of them.

What have we learned that might be adopted in other areas?

The contributors to this book provide a number of learning points for other practitioners and offer a number of suggestions for methods of working that may be usefully replicated elsewhere. These are:

- Development of outreach and drop-in services for 'out-of-hours' provision.
- The development of 'therapeutic outreach'.
- The need to build 'inclusive' services that can respond to the needs of both young men and young women involved in commercial sexual exploitation.
- The need for non-judgemental and non-discriminatory services.
- The need for joined-up services that see the child holistically.
- The need to engage and support children while at the same time devising strategies through which adult abusers can be targeted without relying on the child to give evidence in court.
- The need not to make assumptions about how or why the young person has become involved and to employ different strategies of working depending on how and why involvement occurs.
- The need to support practitioners.
- The need for practitioners to share experience and expertise and have clearly defined protocols to enable them to do so.

Future challenges

There is obviously also a very real need for more resources to be devoted to this area of work to enable partnership working to develop and consolidate. Many of the projects described have short-term funding arrangements. This is evidently not appropriate for young people in need of intensive support over the long term and could even be described as irresponsible or immoral. If projects have worked successfully to engage young people, then financial support for those projects needs to be secured for the long term. If long-term funding is not forthcoming, the danger is that the project will close, highly committed and skilled personnel will change and the young people will be left without support and feeling that they have been let down by yet another agency.

In order to secure resources at an appropriate level to support this work, this area of practice needs to be 'mainstreamed'. There are a number of ways in which this might be achieved. The issue of young people who are sexually exploited through prostitution could be incorporated into local Crime and Disorder Strategies. This would ensure that the work is prioritised in local communities and would receive the resources necessary to tackle it. Additionally, this work could be mainstreamed through the school curriculum, the work of youth services, health services and social services. In the case of the latter, there would be a need to develop services that specifically provide for these young people – for example, provisions for out of area placements when these might be needed.

The government has taken an enormous step in acknowledging that this problem exists in contemporary Britain and in developing guidelines to deal with it. Now it needs to put its money where its mouth is and make adequate resources available to a variety of agencies so that it can be tackled efficiently and appropriately.

Our intention in producing this book has been to develop and inform best practice with young people involved in commercial sexual exploitation. The book demonstrates how to accomplish work with these young people and provides different models for other practitioners to draw on, develop and implement in their own areas. This is a first in this field of practice and we hope that practitioners will find it a valuable tool. We have seen that there is a need for statutory and voluntary organisations to work together in order to achieve effective interventions. Partnerships between managers, practitioners and researchers need to 'make a difference' as they have in the areas from which these contributions have come.

More of the sorts of projects and good practice that have been described in this book need to be developed across the country. These projects need to see the young people with whom they are concerned holistically and provide them with joined-up and seamless services over the long term.

The contributions to this volume demonstrate that our understandings of how best to respond to these young people have developed enormously in a relatively short space of time.

Recommendations

Despite the developments in our knowledge and understandings of this issue, we have already noted that the prevailing socio-economic conditions are ripe for increasing numbers of young people to become involved in commercial sexual exploitation and for the trade in young flesh to flourish (Melrose and Brown, 2002). Below we offer some recommendations that may help to address this problem in future. Some of these have been voiced previously (see Barrett, 1997; Melrose et al., 1999; Barrett, 2000) and this merely demonstrates that commentators must be persistent in trying to get these messages across – especially in the face of institutional denial.

Law and policing

- The Sexual Offences Act 1959 should be amended to be consistent with The Children Act 1989.
- The men involved in abusing young people through prostitution – whether by paying for their 'services' or by forcing them to 'work' need to be vigorously pursued by the police. When they are prosecuted, the sentencing tariffs need to reflect the severity of the crimes in which they have been involved.
- The use of Child Abduction Laws and issuing letters to men involved with young women should become more widespread so that vulnerable young people do not have to make a complaint before action is taken.
- Every effort should be made to achieve prosecutions without the young person having to appear in court to give evidence.
- Effective Missing Persons schemes need to be established in order to identify young people who are most vulnerable.
- Anti-Social Behaviour Orders (ASBOs) should not be used inappropriately for young people involved in prostitution.
- Young people who are trafficked – whether within or across national boundaries – need appropriate welfare responses and the law needs to be developed to ensure that those involved in trafficking them are punished appropriately. The case of a 15-year-old who had been trafficked and abused through prostitution in six European countries before arriving in Britain should shame us all. Prosecutors in Britain could find no law against her having been trafficked as a 'sex slave' and her pimp was only likely to be found guilty of living off immoral earnings. This usually carries a maximum two-year sentence (Kennedy et al., 2002).

Education

- Education and training is needed for a variety of professional groups to raise awareness of the issue and enable professionals to mobilise services already available for young people.

- Education departments should be more proactive with sex education, sexual exploitation and sexual health issues in the curriculum.
- Educators need to recognise more fully their statutory obligations in child protection and be vigilant about their pupils' lives. This means following up absences and making every effort to reduce school exclusions. There is a need for early intervention when problems arise in the classroom.
- Facilities for learning away from the school environment should be provided when necessary.

Drugs

- Coherent services need to be developed for young people experiencing substance misuse problems – currently there is a paucity of such services across the country.
- Every effort must be made to tackle the widespread availability of drugs such as heroin and crack/cocaine on our streets.
- Preventative work in schools needs realistically to confront the dangers of 'those drugs that do the most harm' (President of the Council, 1998) – i.e. heroin and crack/cocaine.

Health

- Young people involved in commercial sexual exploitation have numerous health needs as we have seen from the contributions in this book. Provision needs to be made to address sexual, physical, mental and emotional health needs in appropriate settings – for example, by providing for these needs within projects.
- Harm minimisation approaches need to be adopted (for example condoms, safe injecting equipment etc.) until such time as the young people feel ready to move away from the self-destructive behaviour in which they are involved.

Housing

- Although some Foyers have been established, we have seen through some of the contributions in this book that there is a desperate lack of safe, appropriate housing options for young people involved, or at risk of involvement, in commercial sexual exploitation. This too needs to be addressed as a matter of urgency as any gains made through working with them are quickly undone when they are returned to unsafe housing situations.
- The statutory responsibilities of local authorities in terms of their post-care obligations need to be pursued rigorously and in conjunction with local authority housing departments to ensure that vulnerable young people do not end up on the streets.

Poverty and social inequality
- 'Child-hostile' social policies (Mayall, 1997) have been pursued relentlessly by consecutive governments over the past 20 years. These have contributed to the social and economic insecurity of this age group and undermined their capacity for autonomy.
- One in three children in the UK currently live in poverty. These macro-economic forces are implicated in propelling young people into prostitution and trapping them there once they have become involved. We would suggest therefore that social security and housing benefit entitlements should be restored to 16 and 17-year-olds as a matter of some urgency (Melrose et al., 1999).
- All government departments need to recognise the contribution of economic and neighbourhood destabilisation in family breakdown, running away and child prostitution. What is needed is a micro-social approach that adapts to particular local conditions in conjunction with a macro-level approach that tackles the relative poverty of these young people and the families and neighbourhoods from which they come (Melrose and Ayre, 2002).

Research
- There is still an important role for research to play in this developing field. A national overview of the problem is still needed and although this may be methodologically challenging, this is no reason to shy away from it.
- We now have much more empirical evidence to inform us about the needs of these young people – because our understandings of how and why they become involved in prostitution have been enhanced, we are now in a better position to respond to them appropriately in practice.
- We need to understand more fully the operation and organisation of trafficking networks – both national and international – and develop our responses both to the young people and the men concerned.

The above indicates urgent areas for action by central and local government but of course to implement these changes, political will is required. Until that political will is found the practitioners who have contributed to this book will always be, to some extent, struggling against the tide.

Bibliography

Adams, N., Carter, C., Carter, S., Lopez-Jones, N. and Mitchell, C. (1997) Demystifying Child Prostitution: A Street View, in Barrett, D. (Ed.) *Child Prostitution in Britain: Dilemmas and Practical Responses*. London, The Children's Society.

Aggleton, P. (1999) (Ed.) *Men Who Sell Sex: International Perspectives on Male Prostitution HIV/AIDS*. Philadelphia, Temple University Press

Aitchison, P. and O'Brien, R. (1997) Redressing the Balance: The Legal Context of Child Prostitution, in Barrett, D. (Ed.) ibid.

Altman, D. (1999) Foreword in Aggleton, P. (Ed.) *Men Who Sell Sex: International Perspectives on Male Prostitution and HIV/AIDS*. Philadelphia, Temple University Press.

Ayre, P. and Barrett, D. (2000) Young People and Prostitution: An End to the Beginning? *Children and Society*. 14: 48–59.

Barnard, M., McKeganey, N. and Bloor, M. (1990) A Risky Business. *Community Care*. 5th July.

Barnardo's (1998) *Whose Daughter Next? Children Abused Through Prostitution*. Essex, Barnardo's.

Barrett, D. (1995) Child Prostitution, *Highlight*. No. 135, National Children's Bureau.

Barrett, D. (Ed.) (1997) *Child Prostitution in Britain: Dilemmas and Practical Responses*. London, The Children's Society.

Barrett, D. (1998) Young People and Prostitution: Perpetrators in our Midst. *International Review of Law, Computers and Technology*. 12: 3 475–86.

Barrett, D. (Ed.) (2000) *Youth Prostitution in the New Europe*. Lyme Regis, Russell House Publishing.

Barrett, D. and Melrose, M. (2003) Courting Controversy: Children Sexually Abused Through Prostitution: Are They Everybody's Distant Relatives But Nobody's Children? *Child and Family Law Quarterly*. 15: 4.

Barry, K. (1979) *Sexual Slavery*. New York, New York University Press.

Barter, K. (2001) Building Community: A Conceptual Framework for Child Protection. *Child Abuse Review*. 10: 262–78.

Benson, C. and Matthews, R. (1995) Street Prostitution: Ten facts in Search of a Policy. *International Journal of Sociology of Law*. 23: 4 395–415.

Berridge, D. and Brodie, I. (1998) *Children's Homes Revisited*. London, Jessica Kingsley.

Bluett, M., Walker, A., Goodman, J. and Adeyemo, J. (2000) *Somewhere Safe: Accommodation Needs of Children and Young People at Risk on the Street*. London, The Children's Society.

Boyle, S. (1994) *Working Girls and their Men*. London, Smith Gryphon.

Brain, T., Duffin, T., Anderson, S. and Parchment, P. (1998) *Child Prostitution: A Report on the ACPO Guidelines and the Pilot Studies in Wolverhampton and Nottinghamshire*. Gloucestershire Constabulary.

Brodie, I. (1998) Exclusion from School. *Highlight*. No.161. London, National Children's Bureau.

Brown, A. and Barrett, D. (2002) *'Knowledge of Evil': Child Prostitution and Child Sexual Abuse in Twentieth Century England.* Devon, Willan Publishing.

Brown, L. (2000) *Sex Slaves: The Trafficking of Women in Asia.* London, Virago Press.

NSPCC *Child's Guardian. NSPCC Supporters' Magazine,* London, NSPCC.

Browne, K. and Falshaw, L. (1998) Street Children in the UK: A Case of Abuse and Neglect. *Child Abuse Review.* 7: 241–53.

Christian, J. and Gilvarry, E. (1999) Specialist Services: The Need for a Multi-Agency Partnership. *Drug and Alcohol Dependence.* 55: 265–74.

Cockrell, J. and Hoffman, D. (1989) Identifying the Needs of Boys at Risk in Prostitution. *Social Work Today.* 18 May.

Collison, M. (1996) In Search of the High Life: Drugs, Crime, Masculinities and Consumption. *British Journal of Criminology.* 36: 3 428–44.

Coombs, N. R. (1974) Male Prostitution: A Psychosocial View of Behaviour. *American Journal of Orthopsychiatry.* 44: 782–9.

Craine, S. (1997) The 'Black Magic Roundabout': Cyclical Transitions, Social Exclusion and Alternative Careers, in MacDonlad, R. (Ed.) *Youth, 'the Underclass' and Social Exclusion.* London, Routeldge.

Crawford, A. (1998) *Crime Prevention and Community Safety: Politics, Policies and Practices.* London, Longman.

Crosby, S., and Barrett, D. (1999) Poverty, Drugs and Youth Prostitution: A Case Study of Service Providers' Practical Response, in Marlow, A. and Pitts, J. (Eds.) *Managing Drugs and Young People.* Lyme Regis, Russell House Publishing.

Davis, N. (1981) Prostitutes, in Rubington, E. and Weinberg, M. S. (Eds.) *Deviance: The International Perspective.* New York, Macmillan.

D'Cruze, S. (1998) *Crimes of Outrage: Sex, Violence and Victorian Working Women.* London, UCL Press.

Dean, H. (1997) Underclassed or Undermined? Young People and Social Citizenship, in MacDonald, R. (Ed.) op. cit.

Dean, H. (Ed.) (1999) *Begging Questions: Street Level Economic Activity and Social Policy Failure.* Bristol, The Policy Press.

Dean, H. and Melrose, M. (1996) Unravelling Citizenship: The Significance of Social Security Benefit Fraud. *Critical Social Policy.* 48: 16, 3.

Dean, H. and Melrose, M. (1997) Manageable Discord: Fraud and Resistance in the Social Security System. *Social Policy and Administration.* 32: 2.

Dean, H. and Melrose, M. (1999) Easy Pickings or Hard Profession? Begging as an Economic Activity, in Dean, H. (Ed.) ibid.

De Graff, R., Vanwesenbeeck, I., Van Zessen, G., Straver, C.J. and Visser, J.H. (1995) Alcohol and Drug Use in Heterosexual and Homosexual Prostitution, and its Relation to Protection Behaviour. *AIDS Care.* 7: 35–47.

Department of Health (1991) *The Children Act 1989.* London, HMSO.

Department of Health (1999) *Working Together to Safeguard Children,* London, HMSO.

Department of Health (2000) *Framework for Assessing Children in Need and their Families,* London, Department of Health.

DoH/HO/DfEE (2000) *Safeguarding Children Involved in Prostitution: Supplementary Guidance to Working Together to Safeguard Children.* London, Department of Health.

Department of Health, Home Office (2001) *National Plan for Safeguarding Children from Commercial Sexual Exploitation.* Northern Ireland Office.

Dodsworth, J. (2000) *Child Sexual Exploitation/Child Prostitution. Social Work Monographs. 178,* Norwich UEA.

Doezema, J. (1999) Loose Women or Lost Women. *Gender Issues.* 18: 1, 23–50, accessed at: www.walnet.org/csis/papers/doezema-loose.html

Donovan, K. (1991) *Hidden from View: An Exploration of the Little Known World of Male Prostitutes in Britain and Europe.* Home Office and West Midlands Police.

Duffin, T. L. (1999) *Review of Wolverhampton Pilot Project.* (Unpublished) West Midlands Police.

Duffin, T. and Beech, R. (2000) Implementing Local Protocols: The Experience of the Police in Implementing Association of Chief Police Officers Guidelines on Dealing With Children Abused Through Prostitution. Paper presented at *Barnardo's Awareness to Action Conference,* London, February.

Edwards, S. (1991) *Report on Street Prostitution in Wolverhampton.* (Unpublished) University of Buckingham.

Ennew, J., Gopal, K., Heeran, J. and Montgomery, H. (1996) *Children and Prostitution: How Can We Measure and Monitor the Commercial Sexual Exploitation of Children?* Cambridge, Centre for Family Research and Oslo, Childwatch International.

Farmer, E. and Pollock, S. (1998) *Sexually Abused and Abusing Children in Substitute Care. Caring for Children Away from Home: Messages from Research.* Department of Health, Chichester, John Wiley and Sons.

Faugier, J. and Cranfield, S. (1994) *Making the Connection: Health Care Needs of Drug Using Prostitutes.* Department of Nursing, University of Manchester.

Faugier, J. and Sergeant, M. (1997) Boyfriends, 'Pimps' and Clients, in Scambler, G. and Scambler, A. (Eds.) *Rethinking Prostitution: Purchasing Sex in the 1990s.* London, Routledge.

Fekete, L. and Webber, F. (1997) The Human Trade. *Europe: The Wages of Racism, Race and Class.* 39: 1, 67–74.

Friedberg, M. (2000) 'Damaged Children to Throwaway Women: From Care to Prostitution', in Radford, J., Friedberg, M. and Harne (Eds.) *Women, Violence and Strategies for Actions: Feminist Research, Policy and Practice.* Buckingham, Open University Press.

Foster, C. (1991) *Male Youth Prostitution,* Social Work Monographs. Norwich, UEA.

Frischer, M., Haw, S., Bloor, M., Goldberg, D., Green, S., McKeganey, N. and Coveel, R. (1993) Modelling the Behaviour and Attributes of Injecting Drug Users: A New Approach to Identifying HIV Risk Practices. *The International Journal of Addictions.* 28: 129–52.

Gibson, B. (1995) *Male Order: Life Stories From Boys Who Sell Sex.* London, Cassell.

Gillick, V. (1996) in Powell, R. (2001) *Child Law.* Winchester, Waterside Press.

Gorham, D. (1978) The 'Maiden Tribute of Modern Babylon' Re-Examined. Child Prostitution and The Idea of Childhood in Late-Victorian England. *Victorian Studies.* 21: 353–79.

Green, A., Maguire, M. and Canny, A. (1999) *Keeping Track: Mapping and Tracking Vulnerable Young People*. Bristol, The Policy Press.

Green, J. (1992) *It's No Game*. Leicester, National Youth Agency.

Green, J., Mulroy, S., O'Neill, M. (1997) Young People and Prostitution From A Youth Service Perspective, in Barrett, D. (Ed.) Op. Cit.

Groocock, V. (1992) Streets Ahead. *Social Work Today*. 23: 5.

The Guardian (2002) 26th January.

Hansard Parliamentary Debates.

Hendrick, H. (1994) *Child Welfare, England 1872–1989*. London, Routledge.

Hendrick, H. (1997) *Children, Childhood and English Society*. Cambridge, Cambridge University Press.

Home Office (2002) *Protecting the Public: Strengthening Protection Against Sex Offenders and Reforming the Law on Sexual Offences*. CM5668, London: The Stationery Office.

IPES (2004) International Police Executive Symposium, Eleventh Annual Meeting: *The Criminal Exploitation of Women and Children*. Vancouver, Canada 16–20 May.

Irwin, M.W. (1996) 'White Slavery' As Metaphor: Anatomy of a Moral Panic, *The History Journal*. V: Accessed at: www.walnet.org/csis/papers/irwin-wslavery.html

Ivison, I. (1997) *Fiona's Story: A Tragedy of Our Times*. London, Virago.

Jackson, L. (2000) *Child Sexual Abuse in Victorian England*. London, Routledge.

James, J. (1976) Motivations for Entrance Into Prostitution, in Crites, L. (Ed.) *The Female Offender*. Lexington Mass., Lexington Books.

Jeffreys, S. (1985) *The Spinster and Her Enemies: Feminism and Sexuality 1880–1930*. London, Pandora.

Jesson, J. (1991) *Young Women in Care: The Social Services Care System and Juvenile Prostitution*. Birmingham City Council, Social Services Department.

Jesson, J. (1993) Understanding Adolescent Female Prostitution: A Literature Review. *British Journal of Social Work*. 23: 5, 517–30.

Jones, G. (2002) *The Youth Divide*. York, Joseph Rowntree Foundation.

Kelly, L. and Regan, L. (2000) *Stopping Traffic: Exploring the Extent of and Responses to, Trafficking in Women for Sexual Exploitation in the UK*. Police Research Series, Paper 125, London, Home Office.

Kennedy, D., Tendler, S. and Phillips, J. (2002) Albanian Gangs Corner Britain's Sex Trade. *The Times*. July 6th .

Kershaw, S. (1999) Sex for Sale: A Profile of Young Male Sex Workers' Circumstances, Choices and Risks. *Youth and Policy*. 63, Spring.

Kinnel, H. (1991) *Prostitutes' Experiences of Being in Care: Results of a Safe Project Investigation*. Birmingham Community Health Trust, Safe Project.

Kirby, P. (1995) *A Word From the Street: Young People Who Leave Care and Become Homeless*. London, Centrepoint/Community Care/Reed Business Publishing.

Kohn, M. (2001) *Dope Girls: The Birth of the British Drug Underworld*. London, Granta Books.

Kotter, J. P. (1995) Leading Change: Why Transformation Efforts Fail. *Harvard Business Review*. March–April, 59–67.

Lee, M. and O'Brien, R. (1995) *The Game's Up*. London, The Children's Society.

Lee, R. (1993) *Doing Research on Sensitive Topics*. London, Sage.

Lehti, M. (2003) *Trafficking in Women and Children in Europe*. Heuni Papers No. 18. The European Institute for Crime Prevention, Affiliated With The United Nations.

Linehan, T. (1999) *Pollution and Purification: Child Prostitution and the Age of Consent in Late Victorian England*. MA Dissertation, The LSE.

London Borough (1994) *Tower Hamlets: Education and Community Services, Quality and Equity: Living in Tower Hamlets: A Survey of The Attitudes of Secondary School Pupils*. London, London Borough of Tower Hamlets.

Mahood, L. (1995) *Policing Gender, Class and Family, England 1850–1940*. London, UCL Press.

Matthews, P. (2000) *A Review and a Way Forward: A Report on the Sexual Exploitation of Boys and Young Men*. London, Barnardo's.

May, T. Edmunds, M. Hough, M. and Harvey, C. (1999) *Street Business: The Links Between Sex and Drug Markets*. Police Research Series, Paper 118, London, Home Office.

May, T., Harocopus, A. and Hough, M. (2000) *For Love or Money: Pimps and the Management of Sex Work*. Police Research Series, Paper 134, London, Home Office.

Mayall, B. (1997) Risky Childhoods and Societal Responses. *Risk and Human Behaviour Newsletter*. Issue 2.

McKeganey, N. and Barnard, M. (1996) *Sex Work on the Streets*. Buckingham, Open University Press.

McMullen, R. (1987) Youth Prostitution: A Balance of Power. *Journal of Adolescence*. 10: 35–43.

McMullen, R. (1988) Boys Involved in Prostitution. *Youth and Society*. 23: 35–42.

McNeish, D. (1998) An Overview of Agency Views and Services Provision for Young People Abused Through Prostitution, in *Whose Daughter Next? Children Abused Through Prostitution*. Essex, Barnardo's.

Melrose, M. (2000a) *Fixing It? Young People, Drugs and Disadvantage*. Lyme Regis, Russell House Publishing.

Melrose, M. (2000b) Globalisation and Child Prostitution in Britain in The 1990s. Paper Presented at *The Globalisation of Sexual Exploitation Conference*. London, 10th July.

Melrose, M. (2001) Targeted Groups: Young People Sexually Exploited Through Prostitution, in Factor, F., Chauhan, V. and Pitts, J. (Eds.) *The Russell House Companion to Working With Young People*. Lyme Regis, Russell House Publishing.

Melrose, M. (2002) Labour Pains: Some Considerations of the Difficulties in Researching Juvenile Prostitution. *International Journal of Social Research Theory, Methodology and Practice*. Vol. 5 (4).

Melrose, M. and Ayre, P. (2002) Child Prostitution in the 1980s and 1990s, in Brown, A. and Barrett, D. *Knowledge of Evil: Child Prostitution and Child Sexual Abuse in Twentieth Century England*. Devon, Willan Publishing.

Melrose, M. and Barrett, D. (1999) Not Much Juvenile Justice in These Neighbourhoods: A Report on a Study of Juvenile Prostitution. Paper Presented at *British Criminology Conference*, Liverpool, 13th–16th July.

Melrose, M. and Barrett, D. (2001) Some Reflections on the Contexts, Causes and Responses to Child Prostitution. *Childright*. 174: 10–11.

Melrose, M., Barrett, D. and Marlow, A. (2004) The Flesh Trade in Europe: Trafficking in Women and Children for the Purpose of Sexual Exploitation. Paper Presented at International Police Executive Symposium Eleventh Annual Meeting: *The Criminal Exploitation of Women and Children*. Vancouver: Canada 16–20 May.

Melrose, M. and Brodie, I. (1999) Developing Multi-Agency Responses to Young People Involved in Prostitution. Paper Presented at *Fourth International Conference on the Rights of The Child*, Laval, Quebec, Canada 13th–15th October.

Melrose, M., Barrett, D. and Brodie, I. (1999) *One Way Street? Retrospectives On Childhood Prostitution*, London: The Children's Society

Melrose, M. and Brown, A. (2002) Traffic: Problems in Northern Europe. Paper Presented at Womenaid International UK Anti-Trafficking Network, *Code Red: An Integrated Response to Global Trafficking in Humans*. London, March 10th.

Melrose, M., Greenwood, H. and Barrett, D. (2002) *Highlight*, No. 194. London, National Children's Bureau.

Miller, J. (1995) Gender and Power on the Streets: Street Prostitution in the Era of Crack Cocaine. *Journal of Contemporary Ethnography*. 23: 427–52.

Mort, F. (1987) *Dangerous Sexualities, Medico-Moral Panics in England Since 1830*. London, Routledge and Kegan Paul.

National Vigilance Association Archives, The Women's Library, The University of London.

Nadon, S., Koverola, C. and Schludermann, E. (1998) Antecedents to Prostitution: Childhood Victimisation. *Journal of Interpersonal Violence*. 13: 206–21.

O'Connell-Davidson, J. and Layder, D. (1994) *Methods, Sex and Madness*. London, Routledge.

O'Connell-Davidson, J. (1998) *Prostitution, Power and Freedom*. Cambridge, Polity Press.

O'Neill, M., Goode, N. and Hopkins, K. (1995) Juvenile Prostitution: The Experience of Young Women in Residential Care. *Childright*. No. 113.

O'Neill, M. (2001) *Prostitution and Feminism: Towards a Politics of Feeling*. Cambridge, Polity Press.

Palmer, T. (2001) *No Son of Mine. Children Abused Through Prostitution*. London, Barnardo's.

Patel, G. (1994) *The Porth Project: A Study of Homelessness and Running Away Amongst Vulnerable Black People in Newport, Gwent*. London, The Children's Society.

Pearce, J. and Roach, P. (1997) *Report Into the Links Between Prostitution, Drugs and Violence*. A SOVA (Society of Voluntary Associates) Publication in Collaboration With Middlesex University, Commissioned by Sheffield Drug Action Team, Sheffield Prostitution Forum and Sheffield Domestic Violence Forum.

Pearce, J. J. and Stanko, E. (2000) Young Women and Community Safety. *Youth and Policy*. 66: 1–9.

Pearce, J. J., Galvin, C. and Williams, M. (2000a, 2000b) Finding Young People's Voices: Researching With Young Women Exploited Through Prostitution. Papers

One and Two Presented at *33rd Annual Conference, Social Policy Association,* Roehampton, 18th–20th July.

Pearce, J. J. with Williams, M. and Galvin, C. (2003) *It's Someone Taking Part of You: A Study of Young Women and Sexual Exploitation.* York, Joseph Rowntree Foundation.

Pettiway, L. E. (1997) *Workin' It: Women Living Through Drugs and Crime.* Philadelphia, Temple University Press.

Phoenix, J. (2001) *Making Sense of Prostitution.* Basingstoke, Palgrave.

Phoenix, J. (2002) In the Name of Protection: Youth Prostitution Policy Reforms in England and Wales. *Critical Social Policy.* 71: 353–75.

Pitts, J. (1997) Causes of Youth Prostitution: New Forms of Practice and Political Responses, in Barrett, D. (Ed.) Op. Cit.

Pitts, J. (2001) *The New Politics of Youth Justice: Discipline or Solidarity.* Basingstoke, Palgrave.

President of The Council (1998) *Tackling Drugs to Build a Better Britain: The Government's Ten Year Strategy for Tackling Drug Misuse.* Cm 3945, April.

Rees, G. and Smeaton, E. (2001) *Child Runaways: Under 11s Running Away in The UK.* London, The Children's Society.

Sangera, J. (1998) In the Belly of the Beast: Sex Trade, Prostitution and Globalisation. *Re/Productions* 2, Accessed at: www.hsph.harvard.edu/organizations/healthnet/sasia/repro2

Scambler, G. and Scambler, A. (Eds) (1997) *Rethinking Prostitution: Purchasing Sex in the 1990s.* London, Routledge.

Schissel, B. and Fedec, K. (1999) The Selling of Innocence: The Gestalt of Danger in the Lives of Youth Prostitutes. *Canadian Journal of Criminology.* January, 33–56.

Schorr, L. (1989) *Within Our Reach.* New York, Doubleday.

Seng, M. (1998) Child Sexual Abuse and Adolescent Prostitution: A Comparative Analysis. *Adolescence.* 24: 95 665–75.

Shaw, I., Butler, I., Crowley, A. and Patel, G. (1996) *Paying the Price? Young People and Prostitution.* Cardiff University, School of Social and Administrative Studies.

Shaw, I. and Butler, I. (1998) Understanding Young People and Prostitution: A Foundation for Practice? *British Journal of Social Work.* 28: 177–96.

Sinclair, I., and Gibbs, I. (1998) *Children's Homes: A Study in Diversity.* Chichester, Wiley.

Skidmore, P. (1999) *Nottingham Child Prostitution Project: Report to the Policing and Reducing Crime Unit.* (Unpublished) Nottingham.

Skidmore, P. (2000) *Researching Youth Prostitution,* London, Guildhall University

Smart, C. (1998) *The Historical Struggle Against Child Sexual Abuse, 1910–1960.* Occasional Paper, The University of Leeds.

Stein, M., Frost, N. and Rees, G. (1994) *Running the Risk: Young People on the Streets of Britain Today.* London, The Children's Society.

Stroud, J. (1974) *Thirteen Penny Stamps, The Story of the Church of England Children's Society (Waifs and Strays) From 1881 to the 1970s.* London, Hodder and Stoughton.

Swann, S. (1998) A Model for Understanding Abuse Through Prostitution, in Van Meeuwen, A. *Whose Daughter Next? Children Abused Through Prostitution.* Essex, Barnardo's.

Taylor, G. (2004) Victims of Trafficking in the UK: A Pilot Project. Paper Presented at IPES Eleventh Annual Meeting, *The Criminal Exploitation of Women and Children*. Vancouver, 16–20 May.

Thompson, A. (1995) Abuse by Another Name. *Community Care*. 19th–25th October, 16–8.

Van Meeuwen, A. (1998) *Whose Daughter Next? Children Abused Through Prostitution*. Essex, Barnardo's.

Walkowitz, J. (1992) *City of Dreadful Delight: Narratives of Sexual Danger in Late-Victorian London*. London, Virago Press.

Weeks, J. (2002) Bangkok the New Vienna. *The Times Higher*. March 1st .

Weisberg, D. (1985) *Children of the Night: A Study of Adolescent Prostitution*. Massachusetts, Lexington Books.

Weitzer, R. (Ed.) (2000) *Sex for Sale: Prostitution, Pornography and the Sex Industry*. New York, Routledge.

Wellard, S. (1999) Exit Strategy. *Community Care*. 11th–17th February, 22–3.

West, D. J. and De Villiers, B. (1992) *Male Prostitution: Gay Sex Services in London*. London, Duckworth.

Whitehouse, L. (1991–98) *Annual Reports of Wolverhampton Vice Squad*. (Unpublished) West Midlands Police.

Widom, C.S. and Ames, M.A. (1994) Criminal Consequences of Childhood Sexual Victimisation. *Child Abuse and Neglect.* 18: 303–18.

Yates, G.L., Mackenzie, R.G., Pennbridge, J. and Swofford, A. (1991) A Risk Profile Comparison of Homeless Youth Involved in Prostitution and Homeless Youth Not Involved. *Journal of Adolescent Health*. 12: 545–8.